PRAISE FOR
BUILDING THE BEST

"In *Building the Best*, John Eades has put together a thorough and thoughtful guide to leading. It is a treasure trove of practical wisdom."

> —**Patrick Lencioni**, CEO, The Table Group, and bestselling
> author of *The Five Dysfunctions of a Team* and *The Advantage*

"You will find John Eades has much to share about leadership and life. Readers won't just walk away thinking about how to be a better leader but will have practical tools to help them make it a reality."

> —**Jon Gordon**, bestselling author of *The Energy Bus* and
> *The Power of Positive Leadership*

"John Eades is a student of leadership. His relentless pursuit of the truth over many years has led him to discover the secrets of the most effective leaders. *Building the Best* is an awesome tool to empower you—not only with what he's learned but how you can apply those learnings along your leadership journey."

> —**John O'Leary**, #1 national bestselling author of *On Fire*

"*Building the Best* is smart, interesting, and a fantastic read! I recommend it to any person in management ready to take their leadership to the next level!"

> —**Bob Beaudine**, president and CEO, Eastman & Beaudine,
> and bestselling author of *The Power of WHO!* and *2 Chairs*

BUILDING
THE
BEST

BUILDING
THE
BEST

8 PROVEN LEADERSHIP
PRINCIPLES TO
ELEVATE OTHERS
TO SUCCESS

JOHN EADES

New York Chicago San Francisco Athens London Madrid
Mexico City Milan New Delhi Singapore Sydney Toronto

1 2 3 4 5 6 7 8 9   LCR   24 23 22 21 20 19

ISBN: 978-1-260-45816-9
MHID: 1-260-45816-4

e-ISBN: 978-1-260-45817-6
e-MHID: 1-260-45817-2

Library of Congress Cataloging-in-Publication Data

Names: Eades, John G., author.
Title: Building the best : 8 proven leadership principles to elevate others
    to success / John Eades.
Description: New York : McGraw-Hill, [2020] | Includes bibliographical
    references and index.
Identifiers: LCCN 2019028630 (print) | LCCN 2019028631 (ebook) |
    ISBN 9781260458176 (ebook) | ISBN 9781260458169 (hardcover)
Subjects: LCSH: Leadership. | Success.
Classification: LCC HD57.7 (ebook) | LCC HD57.7 .E225 2019 (print) |
    DDC 658.4/092—dc23
LC record available at https://lccn.loc.gov/2019028630

McGraw-Hill Education books are available at special quantity discounts to use as premiums and sales promotions or for use in corporate training programs. To contact a representative, please visit the Contact Us pages at www.mhprofessional.com.

To the leaders who get up every
morning and reject the notion of making
their life all about themselves.
This world needs you more than ever.

Contents

Acknowledgments

Books aren't written by one person, and careers aren't built by one person either. There are so many people to acknowledge it would take up every page of this book. So if I left you out, thank you.

Thank you to my wife, Amy. When you start to think about how many people there are in the world and how I got so lucky to end up with you as my wife, it's scary. These pages would never have been written without your belief in me and my professional mission. I can't wait for the world to read the work of the real writer in our family.

Thank you to my kids, John Ellis and Lucy. The day you came into my life a purpose was born where words wouldn't do it justice. Don't ever forget, you are going to do great and mighty things—go change the world.

Thank you to Keith and Margie, my parents. While life hasn't always been perfect, I couldn't have asked for a better childhood and environment to grow up in. I learned the value of hard work, professionalism, and grit from you, Dad, and I learned service and community from you, Mom—something I couldn't ever thank you both enough for.

Thank you to Michael and David, my brothers. While we will never be as close as we once were because of age and distance, I learned how to compete and persevere from taking it to both of you my whole life. I am proud to share last name Eades with you both.

To Jim, Lisa, Eric and Laura Beth. I have learned incredible lessons from each of you. I am grateful to be a part of your family and honored to be your friends.

• • •

Thank you to Christina Wilder. Without you there is no way this book would have been written. The daily banter and whiteboard sessions to bring the concepts in this book to life are moments I will never forget. Your sense of humor makes me a better human being, and your willingness to challenge my ideas makes me a better professional. From the very beginning, you saw something in me and took a big leap of faith to join me on this journey. For that, I am forever grateful.

Thank you to Mark Houston. Your development as a professional is something I am so proud of, but what I value the most is your character. I appreciate everything you did as a member of the team and can't thank you enough for the sacrifices you made to get where we are trying to go.

Thank you to Gordon Shuford. Because of your tenacity and effort, this book is going to touch the lives of so many people. You're a great man, and I am so happy to have played a small part in your development as a professional.

To all our clients at LearnLoft: Thank you for the trust and belief in us, it means the world.

Thank you to those who were instrumental in helping me write this book:

- Roderic Yapp: You were the seed many years ago, and I respect you more than you know.
- Bryan Wish: You challenged the writing of someone you didn't know well, and for that I am grateful.
- Connie Hawkins: Only God could have brought you in my life, and I can't thank you enough for the constant encouragement.
- Steve Smith: You are an excellent leader, and the lessons you taught me early in my career I have never forgotten.
- Jacquilyn Lavalle: You have a gift with words, and I hope you continue to use it.
- Trevor Byrd: You are one of the smartest people I have ever met, and I couldn't respect you more. Thank you for your help in bringing our research to life.
- To all the guests who have been on the *Follow My Lead* podcast: Your example of leadership and your willingness to share your stories with me have no doubt shaped my life and thinking.
- To Ludovico Einaudi and NEEDTOBREATHE: Without your music, there is no way this book would have been written. I am pretty sure I know your music better than you do at this point.

Thank you to Taylor Mokris, Doug LaBrosse, Devin Drobbin, and Nick Maslanka. Your friendship and constant belief in me has helped more than you will ever know.

Thank you to Armand Brown and Corey Richard. I do my best daily to be a good example for you and not let you down. You are ready—go do big things that go beyond your own glory.

Above all, thank you to God. None of this is possible without you, and I am constantly amazed at how you are using me.

Introduction

They were words I would never forget: "John, I didn't know what I was supposed to be doing, I didn't know where we were going, and I certainly didn't know how I was helping us get there." Years later, I still replay this moment often. It serves as a poignant reminder from a former team member that leadership is not a blind pursuit. This is precisely where the idea for this book began.

The opportunity to transition from a sales role to running a division within the company presented itself to me in 2014. The new role came with the added responsibility of managing other people. After just one year, frustration set in. Like all young, hungry, and eager professionals, I had grandiose ideas and expectations, most of them revolving around my impact on the people I worked with. Much to my surprise, these expectations for my direct reports were not being met, and my influence on these individuals was minimal. I was stuck in quicksand with no immediate relief in sight. So, I did what an inexperienced leader would do: I made changes to the team.

As I prepared to deliver the unfortunate news, I was far from confident. I wondered, was this the quick fix that would catapult my team to success? Was there more to leadership than hiring, firing, and barking out orders? One of the hardest things I have ever done, I delivered the news to my now ex–team member without much confidence. I was utterly crushed by her aforementioned response.

As she left my office, her words made it clear that the problem was not my team, their drive, skills, or even personalities. It was in me and how I was leading.

Be it fate or divine intervention, I have zero doubt that this moment in my life was predetermined; in it evolved my mission to develop myself as a leader, and from then on I kept the words of author and Navy SEAL Jocko Willink close to my head and my heart: "There are no bad teams, only bad leaders."

Soon after this moment in 2014, I founded the company LearnLoft, a business whose mission would be to turn professionals into leaders and create healthier places to work. It started with a few blogs on LinkedIn to share my leadership struggles, which quickly became a weekly routine and began to garner the interest and attention of thousands of readers.

In those early blogs, I felt like a real imposter helping other people become better leaders when I had barely done it successfully myself. To help grow my own knowledge around the topic of leadership, I started a podcast called *Follow My Lead*. The podcast's purpose was to transfer stories and best practices of today's leaders to the leaders of tomorrow, and that's exactly what it did. Much like the blog, the podcast gained a fast following because of the incredible leaders who agreed to come on the show and share their experiences. The weekly practice of interviewing, editing, and pulling out the best lessons for the weekly blog not only caused my confidence as a leader of my own team to skyrocket but laid the foundation for the book you are about to read.

Since the beginning of that journey, my writing has been read by more than 7 million people on LinkedIn, Inc.com, Thrive Global, Training Industry Magazine, Ragan, and CNBC Money. Because of this traction, I was fortunate to be named a "Top Voice in Management & Workplace" by LinkedIn in 2017. The *Follow My Lead* podcast has been downloaded by more than 500,000 listeners, and 40,000 readers subscribe to my weekly leadership newsletter. The writing and the podcast led to thousands of opportunities to help individual managers become leaders through a virtual instructor-led training program called the Ultimate Leadership Academy, as well as partnering directly with organizations to help improve their employees' leadership skills at every level of their company. I share this with you not to impress you, but to impress upon you that I have always felt as if I was learning and applying right along with my readers, listeners, and students. I have always been on the front lines leading my own team, trying to help others do the same. I was able to take what I learned from the best leaders in the country and put it into action.

An organization I'll call Arlington Gas Co. reached out to LearnLoft after realizing there was a dire need in the company for formal leadership training. The organization's current practice was to promote top performers to positions of leadership as a mechanism to retain talented team members. While this practice isn't unlike what most companies do, it was not producing quality leaders; on the contrary, these newly elevated managers found themselves inept at leading others. Arlington Gas Co. was drawn to the simple idea exposed by our research of more than 40,000 organizational leaders and hundreds of interviews. The most important job of a leader today is to elevate others. In order to elevate others, leaders need to use high levels of love and discipline.

My first coaching call was with a leader named Chris. Chris spoke very highly of his leadership skills and ability to manage his team. In fact, he let me know immediately that our services were most likely going to be a waste of time, something he had told his supervisors at Arlington Gas when they hired us. But because it was a company-wide initiative, Chris had no choice but to participate.

Through our Building the Best (BTB) Leader Assessment, Chris's team provided feedback about how he was leading. The results clearly showed that Chris's opinion of himself was vastly different from the opinion his team members had of him. The feedback showed that he was falling short in a number of areas vitally important in leadership. Seeing the forthright commentary from his team was a sobering moment for Chris, and his response foreshadowed the incredible future that he had as a leader. He immediately engaged in our program, making himself vulnerable to the process and the opinions of his team. His willingness to accept criticism allowed him to become one of the best leaders in his company.

I tell this story because of the parallel between it and my own, and our paths to leadership are not unique.

Many professionals have been promoted without any formal leadership training because it was assumed they were born with some kind of magical leadership DNA. Which raises the question: Are leaders born, or are they made?

A study completed by the *Leadership Quarterly* dove into this concept headfirst. It found 26 percent of leadership ability can be attributed to genetics, while 74 percent is learned. Based on this, one may be able to assume that the great leaders of the past that we all know such as Martin Luther King Jr., Abraham Lincoln, Mother Teresa, and Dwight D. Eisenhower were most assuredly born with innate leadership skills. Even with such a safe assumption, leaders must set their sights on developing their skills in order to get better.

While it's clear that leadership skills are primarily learned and developed, leadership in our companies and organizations aren't in a good place. More money is spent on leadership development than any other area of corporate training, yet recent research by the Brandon Hall Group found that 71 percent of organizations feel that their leaders won't be able to lead them into the future. If that wasn't enough, research conducted by the Corporate Executive Board (CEB) shows that 60 percent of new managers fail within the first 24 months of taking a new position; 50 percent of executives fail within the first 18 months; and only 23 percent of people feel they are led well in the workplace.

Not only are the statistics gloomy, but choosing to be a leader, and more importantly an effective leader, is almost countercultural at this point. The gig economy has provided opportunities to simply work for yourself in varying service or entertainment industries where it's more than possible to make a living and only focus on what's important to you, and you alone. It's as if everywhere you turn, our culture is telling each of us to do the things that provide immediate gratification. I have news for you, this isn't leadership. In fact, it's the opposite of leadership.

My goal for this book is to transfer to you the simple idea that the new model of leading successfully is to elevate others. As someone who has found himself face-to-face with an ugly truth, I want to lay out stories and the research, tools, and personal experiences I have collected for your disposal. This book is meant to be an operating manual in how to Build the Best by focusing on elevating others so you can successfully lead in today's environment. While I am more convinced than ever that there is no exact way to lead other people, this book describes the best way I know how.

The ideas, examples, and principles conveyed in this book are most applicable for frontline managers who lead a team at work, but leaders in all walks of life can find them helpful. From company executives to athletic coaches, parents, teachers, and beyond, it is my hope that you take to heart a few of my words during your leadership journey.

The book is laid out in four parts. The first part, "Change Your Heart," is a collection of stories, ideas, and principles to share the real power of leadership and how it's changing in today's world. The second and third parts, "Start with the Fundamentals" and "Balance People and

Performance," present a practical guide to put these ideas and principles into practice. The last part, "Never Forget These," provides some of the most important lessons leaders need in their arsenal to keep them moving forward during the challenging times.

Here we go . . .

PART I

CHANGE YOUR HEART

1

POINT TO
THE BENEFITS

*"Don't worry when you are
not recognized, but strive to
be worthy of recognition."*
—ABRAHAM LINCOLN

The world spun into a palpable state of shock. While there was deep opposition to his greatest achievements, this was not the way the president was supposed to die. When John Wilkes Booth entered Ford's Theatre on April 14, 1865, the implications of his actions were the last thing on his mind. Stirring up more emotion than patrons had anticipated, Booth approached President Abraham Lincoln from behind, firing his Philadelphia Deringer. The following morning on April 15, Lincoln was pronounced dead, the first US president to be assassinated.

In the weeks that followed, a series of events were held, mourning the president's untimely passing and memorializing his valiant life. More than 7 million citizens paid their respects as Lincoln's body was transported from Washington, DC, to Springfield, Illinois. The political turmoil dissipated as individuals from all walks of life rallied in droves to pay their respects. A good friend and confidant of Lincoln, Ulysses S. Grant, famously wept at one of his memorial services as he said, "Lincoln was the greatest man I had ever known." The heart of the United States was wholly broken.

While the size of one's funeral does not by any means make one a great leader, there is much to be said about the sheer number of people who go out of their way to pay their respects. The impact that a great leader has on the world is powerful enough to set aside the most irreconcilable differences. Like all things, there are two sides to every coin. If great leadership can be powerful enough to set aside irreconcilable differences, what is the impact of being a bad leader?

There are two main costs of being a bad leader: financial and health. The financial cost of being a bad leader varies, but in our research at LearnLoft, we estimate one bad leader costs a company between $100,000 and $115,000 over the course of a year due to higher than average turnover, low employee engagement, and an overall lack of productivity.

The health costs are even more interesting. In 2011, the American Institute of Stress conducted a study on managers and executives, finding that they are 52 percent more likely to die earlier than their counterparts due to stress-related issues. It makes a convincing case that the worse a leader is, the higher the leader's stress is going to be, increasing the likelihood of early death.

If there is such a huge cost to bad leadership, both monetarily and as it pertains to physical health, the natural question becomes: Why do people choose to be bad leaders?

The answer is complicated but stems from the fact that bad leadership is not an isolated issue. Like a plague, it is passed along to everyone it comes in contact with. As up-and-coming leaders look for someone to emulate, they will naturally draw from their personal experiences of being led. If the only example these new leaders have is a negative one, the probability that they will make the same mistakes while leading are high.

Being the victim of an incompetent, unjust, or bad boss causes many organizations to crumble, as bad habits are transmitted and spread throughout the body of an operation.

Look no further than Enron: once a Wall Street darling, the company and its executive leaders were universally applauded for their work. Through a strange series of events, it was revealed that part of the company was a pipe dream built on bad accounting practices and blatant lies. Overnight, the company evaporated as a result of the sixth largest bankruptcy in US history; Enron investors and employees lost everything.

Although it didn't bring back their money or jobs, justice was eventually served to the executives who had masterminded the operation. Founder Ken Lay was found guilty of 10 counts of securities fraud and died shortly after. Allen Fastow, Enron's former CFO, spent six years in prison, and Jeff Skilling, the former CEO, was sentenced to pay $45 million and spend 24 years (later reduced to 14 years) in prison.

While bad leadership is fairly evident in the situation at Enron, Skilling is where the lessons of bad leadership are most prevalent.

Skilling, a Harvard MBA, rose through the ranks at McKinsey & Co. and was noticed by Ken Lay in 1987 during a consulting stint with Enron. He was hired in 1990 as the chief executive officer of Enron Financial Corp. It didn't take long for Skilling's visionary ways and confident style to stand out, eventually he took over as CEO of Enron Corporation when Lay stepped down in 2001.

Skilling's story and management style are well documented in Bethany McLean and Peter Elkind's bestselling book *The Smartest Guys in the Room: The Amazing Rise and Scandalous Fall of Enron*. Skilling was influenced heavily by his experience at Harvard, where professors were required to grade 15 percent of students with a "fail" or "low pass," the two lowest grades possible. He created similar practices within Enron for performance reviews that eventually became known as "rank and yank." This method required every employee to be graded on a 1-to-5 scale with 5 being the lowest. Skilling took a page directly from the administration at Harvard and required that 15 percent of Enron's employees must receive a 5, regardless of their actual performance. Those employees were then given two weeks to find another job within Enron or be terminated.

Skilling believed this unorthodox process was one of the most important in the company because he believed people were only motivated by two things: money and fear. He carried this belief into his personal life, creating the same kind of disastrous effect that imploded his company. He had a nasty divorce in 1997 that caused great strife for his three children and ex-wife. His youngest son, John Taylor, died from a drug overdose in 2011 after Skilling had been in prison for five years. Skilling was a leader who brought the ineffective, extremist style he was accustomed to into his company and his home life, and both failed. What Skilling didn't realize was that replicating the only leadership style he knew was causing his demise.

A recent Gallup study showed that 75 percent of employees leave their jobs because of their bosses and not the position itself. The majority of top performers gladly exit a toxic environment instead of tolerating lousy leadership. This often leaves average or below-average employees reporting to bad leaders. For fear of losing their job, these employees are forced to deal as best they can. A real cyclical effect emerges, and it takes a major shake-up in an organization to change the negative agents at work. Beginning as a small seed that can be easily plucked from the ground, negligent leadership if not addressed it will quickly take hold as a forest.

Your responsibility as a leader is bigger and broader than you think. It reaches far beyond your limited thoughts of the immediate present. Think about the impact Abraham Lincoln, Ulysses S. Grant, and John F. Kennedy had and still have on the world. Conversely, think about the impact Jeff Skilling had on all those who came into contact with him. It's a humbling thought that as a leader, good or bad, you will impact the world for decades after you are gone. Regardless of the leadership you've experienced, the leader that you are and the impact that you will have is a choice that lies within you.

CHAPTER SUMMARY

- The two main costs of bad leadership are financial and health-related.
- Bad leadership is passed on from the actions of bad leaders to the next generation.
- Top performers often don't stand for bad leadership; only average performers do.
- People leave managers not companies.
- You get to choose what kind of leader you want to be.

2

MIRROR WHAT THEY DO

"Leaders aren't born, they are made. And they are made just like anything else, through hard work. And that's the price we'll have to pay to achieve that goal or any goal."

—VINCE LOMBARDI

n 2008, the United States faced one of the biggest financial crises it had ever seen. A 40 percent decline and the collapse of mortgage-backed securities left the economy in a tailspin. Families were in financial hell as homes were being foreclosed at a breakneck speed. President Barack Obama called a state of national emergency as multiple banks and businesses across all industries faced ruin.

A then 32-year-old former professional football player named Casey Crawford saw a major opportunity in the housing industry despite this chaos. He looked on as the Federal Deposit Insurance Corporation (FDIC) closed over 400 failed banks. Crawford guessed that in spite of this, the vast majority of Americans still were going to buy homes over the next 10 years because the inventory of houses wasn't going away. He believed home buyers would demand a different kind of mortgage company, one that would provide confidence and values much different than the companies associated with the collapse. Day in and day out Crawford would pack up his computer and head to the local Starbucks to work on fleshing out his vision and thoughts for a company. On one day in particular, he was explaining the idea to his mentor, Toby Harris. At the end of their discussion, the two men came to a conclusion. Together they would start a company that would help rebuild a decaying industry. These men would build a new kind of mortgage company: one that had the mission of serving customers with a much shorter loan process and would always do what was in the borrower's best interest.

Friends thought he was crazy. Industry experts did not give him the time of day. Even his family was skeptical. Surrounded by doubt and naysayers, Crawford was not deterred from going after his dream. Morning after morning, meeting after meeting, Crawford persevered. His perseverance eventually paid off when a few investors and five mortgage brokers who believed in his vision decided to join him. The New American Mortgage Company was born.

Ten years later, New American Mortgage now goes by the name Movement Mortgage. With over 4,000 employees, the company maintains a simple mission statement: "We exist to love and value people by creating a movement of change in our industry, corporate cultures, and our communities." The company has done an exceptional job of holding true to this promise as positive results flowed through its doors. It became a top 10 loan originator in the United States by 2016 with revenues of $610 million. In addition to its financial success and growth, Movement Mortgage has created industry-changing employee support programs and funded a charter school through its foundation for low-income children in Charlotte, North Carolina. All speak to the accomplishments that go well beyond money and demonstrate the commitment Crawford has to his company's mission statement.

Even When Times Aren't Good

There are many different reasons companies grow and scale. What is special about Movement Mortgage is its dedication to growing a business that does things the right way: by loving and serving people in an industry that commonly did the opposite for its customers. This doesn't happen without a leader like Crawford. His deep and intense focus on building the best and elevating others isn't like the empty words some CEOs tend to use. It is at the core of how he leads, both in times of prosperity and in hardship.

When the marketplace began to put constraints on the mortgage industry with higher mortgage rates and oversaturation of available houses in late 2018, it forced Movement Mortgage to lay off 200 employees. Instead of acting like this was just part of his job and hiding in his office, Crawford showed the remaining employees and those he had to let go what it really meant to elevate others. He called an all hands on meeting and standing in front of the entire company, he called on each and every person to reach out to those who had lost their jobs and let them know they were cared for, thought about, and appreciated for all they had done while at the company. It seemed simple, but to Crawford, it was the only thing to do. He knew that for the company to effectively live out its mission statement of loving and valuing people, it meant not only celebrating the high points in the business but also doing the right things during the low points. He could have left the team on a somber note, but instead, he made sure to let everyone know the future was bright and this was a company that had its brightest days ahead. "This is a company that is going places; one that is playing offense and not defense," said Crawford.

Crawford isn't perfect; no leader is. But he is on a mission to love and value people and build the best through his actions every day, regardless of the circumstances.

● ● ●

It turns out, Crawford isn't alone in leading this way and achieving great results. In 2003, after over a decade of hard work, Jason Lippert had finally earned his big chance. The opportunity to run Lippert Components (LCI) had finally arrived. Founded by his grandfather, Larry, in 1956, LCI had been under the direction of his father, Doug, since 1977. The company was built on the humble idea of manufacturing the best mobile home roofs on the market. By the early 2000s, the business had maneuvered its way through a fair amount of expansion, financial struggles, joint ventures, asset divisions, industry slumps, acquisitions, and a public offering.

LCI was seemingly at its peak when Jason Lippert assumed the role of CEO, hovering around $100 million in sales, since the manufacturing market in America was not exactly seen as the place to be, as many companies outsourced their plants overseas. This was a nondeterrent for Lippert, as he envisioned a new LCI that blew past previous margins and exploded in revenue growth year after year.

From day one in his new role, Jason poured his blood, sweat, and tears into growing the business. He tirelessly proved to not only himself but to the board of directors that putting him at the helm was the right decision. Over the next 10 years, Lippert and his team's relentless efforts paid off in a massive way. The business grew 20 percent each year and amassed revenue of $800 million by 2013. This was the American Dream exemplified. In spite of all of this, however, something did not feel right to Lippert. He would go home each night with a nagging sense that LCI could do more than just turn a profit.

Show Up, Shut Up, Put Up, and Get Out

There was an unspoken code of behavior in the manufacturing industry that had been passed on from decade to decade. Simply put, "you show up, shut up, put up, and get out." Lippert first experienced this mentality when he started at Lippert Components in 1994, fresh out of college. It was commonplace for bosses on the manufacturing line to yell and scream at employees.

Twenty years later, this behavior was still rampant in the business. Even as CEO, Lippert had not made a committed effort to improve it. The revenue and profits were strong, and LCI was growing faster than anyone could imagine. The board was happy, so why rock the boat?

One fateful day, Lippert received an e-mail with a link to a TEDx Talk titled "Truly Human Leadership" by Bob Chapman. Without much thought, he began to watch and quickly became engrossed in the 20-minute video. As he did so, the fog lifted. By the time he had finished watching, it became abundantly clear what was missing in his company. He and his leaders had lost sight of elevating human beings. A shift had to be made to focus on positively impacting the lives of their team members. The present toxic, unspoken code of behavior had to change, and it was going to start right then, with him.

Focus on Others

Despite the growth of the organization, there was a 115 percent turnover rate that was driving inconsistency in the LCI Manufacturing plants. Chapman's talk drew the realization that the high turnover rate could only be blamed on the way LCI leaders treated their team members. Lippert decided he was running the business backward, regardless of what the yearly financial statement said. Employees had to be put first to rebuild things from the inside out.

Chapman had anchored his leadership approach to core values and living them out, so Lippert decided to do the same. His team defined the five core values they would wrap their culture around. These values would drive their attitudes, behaviors, and actions every day, at every facility:

- Passionate About Winning
- Team Play with Trust
- Honesty–Integrity–Candor
- Caring About People
- Positive Attitude

Lippert knew that just announcing the core values or putting them on a wall was not going to instill the change his company needed. He made the choice to visit each LCI facility with one goal in mind: to listen and share. It took no time at all to realize these core values were not present in the LCI workplace at the time. Lippert took action in a big way to show just how serious he was about building the best and elevating others for his 9,000-plus team members.

The company spent millions of dollars upgrading its facilities, providing employees with a clean, safe, and better place to come to work. He formed a Leadership Development department and hired several leadership coaches to serve as trainers, coaches, and trusted advisors that lived, breathed, and worked alongside of leaders at every layer of the organization. It was an approach that did not rely on Lippert's words, but his actions. He did not stop there. Each and every day he took notes as he listened to employees, then turned those notes into actionable items. He implemented employees' ideas throughout the company, complementing them with ones from his executive team. His people did not need to wonder if they mattered; he showed them they did.

It All Starts with a Model

By the middle of 2018, LCI's core values and the Leadership Development department were well entrenched and the business had soared to new heights beyond what Larry, Doug, or even Jason Lippert could have imagined. The results were astounding: annual revenue hit $2.5

billion, employee engagement was at an all-time high, voluntary turnover was at a record low, and they were positively touching the lives of 11,000 employees and their families. It would be convenient to say this was achieved by chance or because LCI is in a great market, but that would not be the truth. The success of LCI began with a leader named Jason Lippert, who wanted more out of his career and life than making parts, generating revenue, and growing for the sake of growing.

Jason Lippert and Casey Crawford are in different industries and lead different businesses, but both exemplify the idea that building the best and elevating others is not only the right thing to do, but it's a key to successful performance. Which begs the question: Can leadership be this simple?

There are some 30,000 different definitions of leadership. Arguably the most popular today comes from John Maxwell: "Leadership is influence." While Maxwell is right that influence is a contributing factor to leadership, it isn't quite that simple. Dwight D. Eisenhower said, "Leadership is the art of getting someone else to do something you want done because he wants to do it." This doesn't quite hit the nail on the head either. A personal favorite of mine, Peter Browning, former CEO of National Gypsum, stated, "Leadership is influencing people towards a worthwhile goal over an extended period of time." Another fantastic interpretation, although it may be difficult for a new leader to identify with. John Quincy Adams, the sixth president of the United States, has been linked to this quote, "If your actions inspire others to dream more, become more, learn more, and do more, you are a leader." Those words were backed up in the modern day by Microsoft founder Bill Gates who said, "As we look into the next century, leaders will be those who empower others."

It is easy to see why there are many ways to define leadership. So many tremendous leaders have left us with their input. The definition I use and teach in our Building the Best workshops is the definition I want you to commit to memory:

> Leadership is inspiring, empowering, and serving
> in order to *elevate others* over an extended period
> of time.

These words are chosen carefully and for great reason. The word *inspire* has its origin from Latin, and it means "to breathe life into." *Empower* means "to give control over another's life and the authority to do something." "Serve" comes from the Latin word *servant*, in modern context it means "to devote (part of) one's life or efforts to others." All three are paramount to building the best and elevating others. If what you are doing to proactively elevate others results in them being more inspired, empowers them to make decisions, and serves their heart, then you are on your way to true leadership. In addition, you must help others move into a more permanent state of improvement.

Crawford and Lippert are people who truly embody this definition of leadership. They have continued to inspire, empower, and serve in order to elevate others, regardless of the situation.

While having an incredible leader at the helm is critical, in order to grow and evolve as a business or team, you must have an army of leaders behind you that also build the best and elevate others. What they need is a simple idea or way to think about how to do it. This is exactly what the rest of this book is all about.

CHAPTER SUMMARY

- Leadership is not about you; it's about inspiring, empowering, and serving in order to elevate others over an extended period of time.
- Leading this way produces excellent business results and builds better people.
- It's important to elevate others regardless of times being good or bad.
- Words are cheap—make leadership about your actions.

3

PRACTICE LOVE AND DISCIPLINE

"The essence of leadership is holding your people to the highest possible standard while taking the best possible care of them."

—COLIN POWELL

Principle 1: Use High Levels of Love and Discipline to Elevate Others

Enthusiastic fans with unrealistic expectations come with the territory of a college football program. Clemson University is no exception to this rule, having a long and storied history complete with a National Championship in 1981, followed by a 15-year period of average achievements. Critics began using the term "Clemsoning" to describe losing to a team of lesser talent regardless if Clemson was involved or not.

Midway through the 2008 season, at what felt like rock bottom to Clemson fans, Coach Tommy Bowden was fired and replaced by Dabo Swinney. An interim choice, Swinney led the Tigers to a 4-3 record to finish the season. Without much luck finding a big-name replacement and a deep belief in an unproven commodity, Clemson's athletic director, Terry Don Phillips, decided to take a chance on the young Swinney by removing his "interim" tag and naming him the permanent head football coach. Phillips recalled, "I liked the way he coached his players, how he was tough on them but was always teaching them and always there for them outside of football. It's not a facade with Dabo. He genuinely cares, and his players sense that."

What transpired over the next 10 years is nothing short of magical. Since Swinney took over not only did Clemson win National Championships in 2016 and 2018, but they have sustained excellence, winning over 79 percent of their games and having nine straight seasons of 10-plus wins. There is no doubt that in 2019, the Clemson Tigers are an elite program, setting the standard for every other college football program in the country.

I spent some time with author and speaker Jon Gordon at a Clemson game late in the 2016 season. Gordon worked with Swinney and knew the football program well. When I asked what made Swinney a standout leader, Gordon's answer was one that I will never forget. He explained, "I have never seen a leader use love and discipline like him." Those words, "love" and "discipline" stuck in my head. As a leader of my own team and a parent to two kids, I understood the struggle in balancing the delivery of both. Over the next few days, I couldn't shake the feeling that there was more to this idea of love and discipline, specifically when it came to building the best and elevating others. The nagging feeling set me and the LearnLoft team on an investigation of the idea.

Specifically, we looked into Swinney himself and found two standout instances in which he effortlessly tied in his use of love and discipline to elevate others. The first occurred with Clemson's 2015 team. They appeared in their first College Football Playoff game in 27 years. The anticipation by fans was palpable! But in the days prior to the big game, Swinney suspended five players including their star wide receiver, Deon Cain. The majority of the Clemson faithful were in disbelief and downright frenzied at the choice. Swinney did not bat an eye. He said publicly that Cain and others chose not to meet the standards set by the Clemson coaching staff and wouldn't get the opportunity to play in the game. If the players had eligibility the next year, they could come back to school and make the choices necessary to be a part of the team, but it wouldn't be that season.

Swinney's act was pure discipline. The standards were set, and those who chose not to live up to the standards were not allowed to play. Clemson lost the game against Alabama, but Swinney stood by his convictions; he knew he had made the right decision because he was serving his players' hearts and not their talents. He knew his job wasn't just to win football games but to build the best men and prepare his players for life after their time at Clemson.

Fast-forward a year later to our second example. The Clemson team found themselves back in the College Football Playoffs, this time in the National Championship game against the University of Alabama. Clemson went on to play one of the most talked-about games in history, coming out victorious. And yes, Deon Cain did return to the team and played a critical role in the game. He caught five passes for 94 yards and made one of the biggest plays in the game late in the fourth quarter to spur a Clemson comeback.

Following the game, a reporter interviewed Swinney. After thanking God, he said, "I told the team at halftime the difference in the game was going to be love." Swinney didn't shy away from using the four-letter word on national television.

While the examples Swinney gave us of both love and discipline in a sports team environment were fantastic, we wondered if the same concept would be applicable in the corporate workplace. Specifically, how could the terms "love" and "discipline" translate into a corporate environment? (They aren't exactly words encouraged by Human Resources.)

We examined the managerial grid model developed in the 1960s by Robert Blake and Jane Mouton. The managerial grid looked at leader effectiveness through the eyes of two critical elements: a concern for people and a concern for production. Blake and Mouton found a direct improvement in leader effectiveness when both a concern for people and concern for production were high. Blake and Mouton's work provided an example for our team as we began studying the concept of love and discipline further. We wanted to see exactly how the best leaders built the best and elevated others and if love and discipline played a role.

Love and *discipline* are words that can be ambiguous, so as we continued our research, we gave them both definitions that apply to the workplace.

> **Love** (verb): to contribute to someone's long-term success and well-being

> **Discipline** (verb): to promote standards in order for an individual to choose to be at his or her best

By using these definitions of *love* and *discipline*, we formed a hypothesis: the most effective leaders who elevate others lead with high levels of love and discipline.

Now, real data was needed to determine if our hypothesis was true in the workplace. We conducted an initial study of 300 leaders in various roles ranging from CEOs to frontline managers. Instead of asking these leaders directly about their current leadership styles, we surveyed those who knew how they led the best: their team members.

We evaluated each leader's effectiveness by averaging responses from the following two statements:

> "Our team consistently meets business goals and objectives."

> "Leadership skills are developed within each individual on our team."

In order to measure love, we asked individuals to rate their leader on four statements using a scale of 1 to 10.

- "My leader is genuinely concerned about my life outside of work."
- "My leader would set me up for a promotion outside of his/her team."
- "My leader spends time coaching me towards my goals."
- "My leader is vulnerable around me."

We asked them to do the same for discipline.

- "My leader is disciplined."
- "My leader encourages team members to be disciplined."
- "My leader has a set of standards for our team."
- "My leader consistently holds those who do not meet standards accountable."

Scores for both love and discipline were calculated using the average of the four scores. We then plotted the two scores on a graph with love on the horizontal axis and discipline on the vertical axis (Figure 3.1). The data revealed a direct correlation between leaders' effectiveness and their use of love and discipline.

FIGURE 3.1 Scores for Love and Discipline for All Leaders

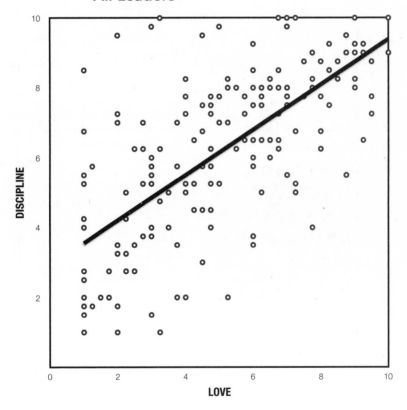

Highly effective leaders were those who leveraged high levels of both love and discipline (Figure 3.2); those leaders who ranked low in effectiveness rated low in their use of love and discipline (Figure 3.3). Our hypothesis was correct!

FIGURE 3.2 Scores for Highly Effective Leaders

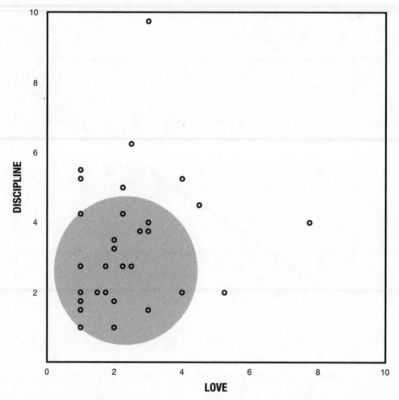

FIGURE 3.3 Scores for Ineffective Leaders

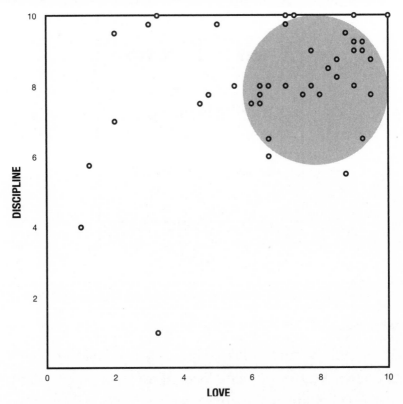

The Five Leadership Styles

More than three years and 40,000 assessments of organizational leaders later, five clear-cut leadership styles
emerged (Figure 3.4). Each related to how well a person
leverages love and discipline when leading others. While
these are *current* styles of leading, they are not meant to
be definitive.

FIGURE 3.4 Five Leadership Styles

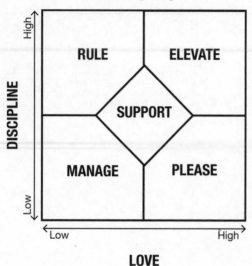

Manage

People whose current leadership style is to manage others are often leaders by title alone. They push people along instead of pulling them up. They focus more on themselves than on the people they are supposed to be leading. Because of that, people work for them rather than follow them.

A person with this style:

- Scores low in areas of love and discipline
- Focuses solely on execution
- Lacks great relationships with team members
- Directs rather than coaches
- Tends to be shortsighted
- Looks at the position as one of power and authority
- Believes he or she makes the best decisions in almost all situations

Rule

People whose current leadership style is to rule others take their position extremely seriously. They value their authority and regulations above relationships with people. The thought of not having control or not being the centralized decision maker makes them uncomfortable. To ensure this does not happen often, leaders who rule others create processes and environments that funnel decision making to them in almost all matters. They tend to come across as heartless because of their reliance on the way things "must" be done.

A person with this style:

- Scores high in discipline, low in love
- Driven by a set rulebook, rigid
- Gets great or bad results quickly
- Has a hard time sustaining success because of team burnout
- Never heard an excuse he or she liked
- Creates process before it's needed
- Has "favorite" team members

Please

People whose current leadership style is to please others are generally not comfortable being in a position of authority. They love people and their job, but they expressly avoid having conflict with team members. They tend to give people too many chances and are often naive about the realities of what is going on around them. Their team members like them as people, but there is a lack of respect for them in a professional capacity.

A person with this style:

- Scores high in love, low in discipline
- Gets taken advantage of by his or her direct reports
- Is often passed over for promotions
- Gets stuck in low levels of organizational leadership for long periods of time
- Treats everyone equally regardless of talent levels
- Leads a team that tends to underperform

Support

People whose current leadership style is to support others are good, not great, leaders. The most popular style to fall into, 47 percent of all leaders from our research currently lead this way. They often have good relationships with their team members and achieve business goals and objectives. They struggle, however, with reaching the next level of success as a leader.

A person with this style:

- Scores in the middle in love and discipline
- Has great relationships with some and average to below-average relationships with others
- Is regarded as a solid contributor in the organization
- Leads a team that performs well but could be better

Elevate

People whose current leadership style is to elevate others simultaneously use high levels of love and discipline. They constantly exceed goals and objectives, have deep relationships with team members, and make a positive impact on the lives of those they lead.

A person with this style:

- Scores high in love and discipline
- Has deep relationships based on mutual respect
- Leads a team that consistently exceeds goals
- Helps create more leaders
- Is often looked at as a mentor and role model
- Often has people seek advice and counsel from him or her

Before you make an assumption about your leadership style, it's important to note that these aren't personality profiles. These leadership styles are meant to serve as a mirror you can hold up to see how you're currently leading. Just because your current leadership style is to rule or elevate today doesn't mean you're stuck with that style for life. You can improve or you can regress because leadership is a journey and not a destination. The best part is that *you* decide how you lead others each and every day. You can take a free assessment to uncover your current leadership style at Buildingthebestbook.com/assessment.

One Clear Winner

As our team continued to study all five leadership styles, we asked leaders who completed the assessment to answer three questions in the context of the past two years:

1. What percentage of your team would you consider high performing?
2. What percentage of your direct reports have been promoted?
3. What percentage of voluntary turnover have you had with your direct reports?

FIGURE 3.5 Elevate vs. All Other Styles

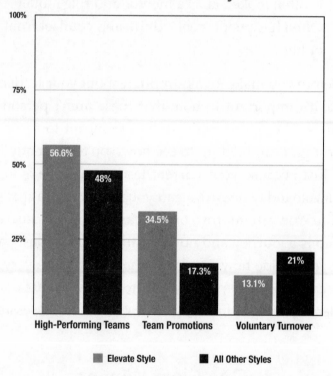

The results continue to prove our hypothesis to be true. Those whose current leadership style is to elevate reported having high-performing teams at rates better than all other teams combined. They reported:

- 14 percent more top performers
- 18 percent more internal promotions of team members
- 11 percent lower voluntary turnover

Those whose style is to elevate outperform all other leadership styles significantly. This realization cemented the idea that building the best requires the use of high levels of love and discipline.

Leaders Whose Leadership Style Is to Elevate Demonstrate These Competencies

Once we identified those leaders whose style is to elevate, we continued to examine their behaviors to uncover how they leverage love and discipline. Sixteen key demonstrable competencies were isolated, eight in love and eight in discipline (Tables 3.1 and 3.2).

These 16 core competencies are a fantastic barometer to determine specific strengths and weaknesses in the way you lead. All of them are weaved into the chapters, models, and principles I'll share with you throughout the rest of the book.

Whether you have taken the full 48-question assessment and received your detailed BTB Leader Report or not, it's important to examine not only what you believe to be your current leadership style, but how well you demonstrate these 16 competencies on the job each day.

TABLE 3.1 Love Competencies

Recognition	How often and effectively you take advantage of opportunities to make your team members feel valued and appreciated.
Personability	How engaging you are with individuals on your team, both in your mannerisms and demeanor.
Development	How much emphasis you put on the development of your team to ensure their long-term success and well-being.
Unity	How well you create a sense of belonging and connections between your team members.
Positivity	How optimistic you are when speaking to or being around your team.
Vulnerability	The level at which you share the truth about mistakes, personal feelings, or lack of knowledge.
Empathy	How well you are able to identify with your team to understand their feelings and perspectives, in order to guide your actions.
Trust	How confident your team is that you will do what's right.

The Power of Knowing Your Leadership Style

After studying, coaching, and teaching thousands of leaders, it's always interesting to see people react to discovering their current leadership style. But the power of the exercise doesn't lie in crowning anyone the greatest leader ever or chastising those who are less than effective. It's meant for one simple and powerful reason: to improve self-awareness. Improving in any skill, leadership included, requires a level of self-awareness that opens the heart and mind to do some things differently.

TABLE 3.2 Discipline Competencies

Standards	How clearly you define, communicate, and promote what good looks like.
Coach	How effective you are at providing guidance and training to improve the skills of your team.
Goals	How clearly you've defined, communicated, and measured goals.
Model	How well you exemplify the standards and behaviors you expect from your team.
Consistency	The stability, predictability, and emotional intelligence of your behaviors.
Accountability	How effectively and consistently you hold your team accountable to the standards you've set.
Priority	How clearly you determine the order in which your team should complete work based on relative importance.
Vision	How well you define, communicate, and reinforce what you want your team or business to be in the future.

A common practice for officers in the Marines is to put together what they refer to as an Iron Council. This group consists of six direct reports and peers of an officer. A few times a year the Iron Council meets with their officer in a group setting to provide feedback about the leader's performance over the past few months. The meeting isn't meant to promote a forum to air petty grievances but rather to provide a constructive place to improve.

Something amazing happens after these Iron Council meetings. While feedback can be tough to hear for most, officers find themselves on a mission to grow and get better. Officers take the opportunity to increase their self-awareness about how they are leading and identify specific things they can do to improve moving forward. When provided with further formal or informal leadership development opportunities, the officers are engaged and take ownership of their education.

Whether you have formed an Iron Council around you or if you have taken the full BTB Leader Assessment and received your individualized report, know that simultaneously leading with high levels of love and discipline isn't easy. But if you don't use love, you won't connect with people to get their best possible performance. If you don't use discipline, you aren't going to get anyone to levels they didn't think possible. If that weren't enough, it's tough to be tough on people, and it's tough to love people when you don't feel like loving them.

Train Your Mind if You Want to Improve

In the Introduction of this book, I highlighted the research done by *Leadership Quarterly* showing that leaders aren't born but instead use a combination of genetics and development. For many people, this is a major change in thinking, but it's the only way to think if you are going to get better from a leadership perspective or, for that matter, anything.

The development of leadership skills isn't just about reading this book or practicing the concepts within it during the rest of your career. Instead, the most important factor, if you want to improve, is changing how you think. It could be summarized as having a growth mindset. The growth mindset theory was brought to prominence by Carol S. Dweck, a Stanford psychology professor. In simple terms, it suggests that "we can grow our brain's capacity to learn and solve problems."

Dweck wrote in her book *Mindset*:

> [The *fixed mindset* believes that your qualities are carved in stone and] it creates an urgency to prove yourself over and over. If you only have a certain amount of intelligence, a certain personality, and a certain moral character— well, then you'd better prove that you have a healthy dose of them. . . . *The growth mindset* is based on the belief that your basic qualities are things you can cultivate through your efforts, your strategies, and help from others. Although people may differ in every which way—in their initial talents and aptitude, interests, or temperament—everyone can change and grow through application and experience. Do people with this mindset believe that anyone can become anything, that anyone with proper motivation or education can become Einstein or Beethoven? No, but they believe a person's true potential is unknown (and unknowable); that it's impossible to foresee what can be accomplished with years of passion, toil, and training.

If there is nothing else you learn from this book, whether you adopt it for yourself or pass it along to your people, wrap your heart and mind around this concept. Not only will you start to see failure as feedback instead of failure being final but you will be growing every day rather than being in neutral or going backward.

We are all born with unique DNA. I started with a different makeup than you did. It might be easier for me to handle pressure than it is for you because of my DNA. But you can still learn how to handle pressure effectively. You might have been born with better leadership DNA than I was, but I can still learn how to be an effective leader.

Unfortunately, the majority of professionals fall into the category of having a fixed mindset over a growth mindset. They fall into the trap of believing that talent wins every time and they were either born with the ability to get the job done or they weren't.

Turns out it isn't limited to professionals; it happens at every age. My six-year-old son is learning how to read. Each night his teacher sends home two lists of sight words to learn and a short book. Early in the school year, I sat down with him to go through the sight words. The first was a list of words like *a, the, with, where, can,* and *was.* We weren't past the third word before my little man broke down in tears saying, "I can't do it." Instead of allowing him to give up, I helped him sound out the next word and gave him positive reinforcement when he said the word correctly. In less than three minutes he got through the list of 30 words. Excited, we moved on to the next block of sight words. Again, we weren't past the third word before my little man broke down in tears saying, "I can't do it." Instead of allowing him to give up, I helped him sound out the next few words followed by an excited "yes!" when he read them correctly. In less than two and a half minutes, he got through the list of 30 words. Next, we moved on to the short book. Again, before we got through the first page, he broke down in tears, crying, "I can't do it." Instead of allowing him to give up, I helped sound out the words, and before long he completed the 13-page book. We both erupted in cheers, and I said, "I knew you could do it!" Afterward, I asked him to share with my wife how the homework went. He said, "I got frustrated with my first list of sight words, but then I tried to sound out each word and I did it. Then with my second set of words, I got frustrated again, but I did it. When we got to the book, I was frustrated and wanted to give up, but I kept sounding out the words and I read a *whole* book by myself!"

Now I share this story not because I believe my son is naturally gifted or because I am naturally gifted as a parent but because all kids come out of the womb not knowing how to read. The way I was able to begin changing my son's mindset about reading from a fixed mindset to a growth mindset was by focusing on the pattern of what happened to him. In each of the three exercises, he wanted to quit when he didn't immediately know the answer but eventually, he completed them successfully. Thus a pattern emerged of action, outcome, learning.

You can focus on a similar pattern for yourself around having a growth mindset in life and around the development of your leadership skills. It's what I call AOL, an acronym that stands for action, outcome, learning (Table 3.3). Let's take my own development as an example. As a leader of a team, my ability to have effective direct dialogue is a critical skill to develop for myself and my team.

TABLE 3.3 AOL Pattern

STEP 1. Action	Conducting a consequential conversation with a team member
STEP 2. Outcome	Experiencing success or failure with the consequential conversation
STEP 3. Learning	Leveraging the outcome to help the next time a consequential conversation takes place

Obviously, this is just one example of AOL in action, but it can be a powerful way to begin making a shift in yourself. Naturally, at this point, you have probably already started to do a brief mental evaluation of whether you have a growth or fixed mindset. While that is fine, I want you to remember that if you currently have a fixed mindset, it doesn't mean you can't change. (Remember my six-year-old learning how to read.) It's your job to ensure you adopt a growth mindset instead of a fixed mindset, and the AOL approach is just one way do that.

Moving from Knowledge to Wisdom

The rest of this book has been designed specifically to help you leverage love and discipline at higher levels and improve your skills in the 16 key leadership competencies to truly build the best and elevate others. I know words in a book mean nothing unless they are put to use because power is not in the knowledge, but rather, the application of knowledge. This became real to me when a mentor of mine shared an important lesson (Figure 3.6):

- Knowledge is information.
- Understanding is comprehension.
- Wisdom is application.

FIGURE 3.6 Steps to Wisdom

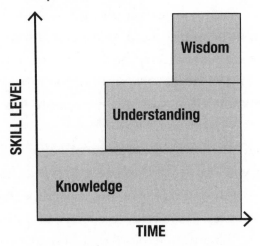

Karl Popper famously said, "True ignorance is not the absence of knowledge but the refusal to acquire it." In today's modern Internet, information is more readily available to more people than at any time in history. Anyone with an Internet connection can find information at little to no cost. That presentation of information is accompanied by the opportunity to comprehend it. Sometimes we can comprehend the information on our own, and other times we might need a teacher, instructor, or expert to help us.

While understanding is an important step, the true test is the ability to apply knowledge. Wisdom and application are supreme as there is so much one could understand, but never apply. A heart surgeon who smokes cigarettes, a diabetic who chooses to eat sugar, or a music student who can read music but cannot play an instrument are all prime examples of comprehending but not applying.

What you should be striving for is gaining a level of wisdom that creates ease of application. I understand this is simple to write and difficult to execute. I have done my best to provide you with the best stories, examples, tools, principles, and resources throughout the rest of the book to transfer knowledge and help you apply it so you can truly elevate others.

Now that you know there is great value in being the best leader you can be, and in order to build the best you have to use high levels of love and discipline, the natural question becomes, "Where do you start, and how do you do it?" We will begin to explore that in the next chapter.

CHAPTER SUMMARY

- Principle 1: Use high levels of love and discipline to elevate others
- The best leaders use love and discipline simultaneously at high levels.
- Love means to contribute to someone's long-term success and well-being.
- Discipline means to promote standards in order for an individual to choose to be at his or her best.
- There are five leadership styles: manage others, please others, rule others, support others, elevate others.
- Training the brain to adopt a growth mindset is a key to getting better.
- Adopt a growth mindset using AOL: action, outcome, learning.
- Knowledge matters, but the application of the knowledge is most important.

PART II

START WITH THE FUNDAMENTALS

4

BUILD
REAL BONDS

"To be trusted is a greater compliment than being loved."
—GEORGE MACDONALD

Principle 2: Without Strong Relationships, You Can't Lead

In recent years, the US military has been in the midst of fighting wars all over the world; its primary target has been Al-Qaeda and ISIS in the Middle East. In 2013, an American general named Robert Caslen was called on by the United States Military Academy to return to his alma mater and serve as the 59th Superintendent of West Point. Not only was this a dream job for him because of what the Academy had done for him in his career, but the position carried a large amount of responsibility and honor. The institution boasted a number of former cadets as accomplished American leaders in their respective fields, such as Dwight D. Eisenhower, Robert E. Lee, Ulysses S. Grant, George Patton, and Edgar Allan Poe.

After he agreed to take the job, Caslen couldn't help but consider the great opportunity in front of him. It was his job to prepare the army's cadets to lead during one of the most difficult times in the country's history. Caslen wasted no time instilling a culture built on rising above mediocrity and adversity in order to protect America at all costs. It didn't take long for the army cadets to revere him; he showed them he loved and respected them while demanding they remained disciplined by a set of principles. During his time there, Caslen instilled and lived out the West Point values of "duty, honor, country" and provided a near perfect model of the Honor Code: "A cadet will not lie, cheat, steal or tolerate those who do."

While doing research for this book , I spent time with General Caslen in order to better understand exactly how the Academy taught its graduating cadets (future army second lieutenants) to build trust with their new teams. Caslen said, "Failing at leadership isn't an option due to the extreme circumstances our 870 second lieutenants are going to face upon graduation. Within a few months, all will be leading troops in battles. Most of the troops each of them will lead, won't even care they went to West Point, some will actually resent that fact they were West Pointers. So once they get there, each soldier will evaluate how much they can trust their new second lieutenants by asking two important questions, Are they competent? Do they care?"

He continued, "Competence is most important because if you aren't competent as a lieutenant of a platoon, you are going to get people killed and they aren't going to go home to their families. So the soldiers are most concerned with competence. Quickly after competence, they evaluate whether the lieutenant really cares about them on a personal and professional level. Competence and care work together because once they know a lieutenant cares they are going to follow them that much closer and it will make them look even more competent. The moral of the story is, trust matters so much because lives are at stake."

The people that you lead at work probably don't have bullets flying at them, but their lives are still at stake. They go to work to provide for their families and desire to do work that matters during the time they have on earth. They have to believe in, and most importantly, trust you as their leader by knowing that you are competent and that you care.

The ability to lead a team starts with good, quality, professional relationships, built on the bond of mutual trust. As a leader, you must consistently share your competence and care in order for people to trust you. The key word here is *consistency*. Reid Hoffman, founder of LinkedIn and partner at Greylock, came up with my favorite formula for easily understanding trust.

$$\text{Consistency} + \text{Time} = \text{Trust}$$

When you break down the simple formula, it makes so much sense. Regardless of how long you have been leading other people, we can all relate to building trust with someone in our lives. Trust is the foundation everything else is built upon, and it's created by consistency over time. Someone doing what they say they are going to do, day in and day out. Falter once, and trust can be damaged. Imagine if General Caslen preached the importance of competence and care, only to fail to carry out his teachings in everyday actions with his cadets. There is no way his methods and guidance would have made such a big difference if Caslen hadn't built trust by living out his own principles.

Reject Your Natural Instincts

One of the leaders I work closely with has a mix of men and women on his team. In our initial coaching conversation, it was clear that he had much stronger, trust-based relationships with the men on his team. As we unpacked the reasons, it was evident he gravitated toward the men because they looked like him, acted like him, and behaved like him. The women on the team were in roles where he had little to no firsthand experience. They didn't talk like him, and they certainly didn't think like him. Through multiple coaching ses-

If you want better trust-filled relationships, look beyond commonalities.

sions, he reached a point of self-realization. He had been playing favorites and putting in more work and effort with the men on the team than the women.

What I now know is that this man isn't in a league of his own. All leaders are challenged to overcome different biases in order to have better trust-filled relationships across their teams. However, our natural instinct as human beings is to gravitate toward and trust people who look, act, or behave like us. This manifests itself in both leaders and their people.

Add in Character

Maria Weist learned a powerful way to earn the trust of others early in her career. Promoted at the age of 25, Maria became the youngest IT manager at her company. Hoping to mitigate potential difficulties, her boss, Arch Humphries, provided some valuable insight.

He said, "It's important to ask yourself this question before you get started in this role: who do you want to be as a leader? It's an important question to answer because there is no doubt you are less experienced and younger than the people you will be leading, but that doesn't mean you can't do the job. Show your character early on by telling them the truth when you don't know something and do everything you can to be a sponge and learn from your team's expertise and experience."

Maria carried Humphries's wise words with her throughout her career by consistently showing her true character. She was always honest and transparent and didn't shy away from treating people fairly, regardless of the situation.

She shared one instance in particular in which her character was put to the test. During a meeting with a woman on her team, Maria pressed her on a project that was not going well. The woman said outright, "I want to leave this conversation, now." Acting on the very obvious cue, Maria told her to step out and take the time she needed. Thirty minutes later, the woman returned. "I can't believe you let me leave. Why did you?" she asked. Maria responded, "I knew it's what was best for you at that moment. I had to put my own interests aside and focus on you because it was the right thing to do." The strong connection Maria built with her teammate allowed for the best-case scenario to occur. For the relationship to work, the trust had to be mutual.

The challenge some leaders face is that they don't give enough weight to the individual relationships and instead think of their relationship with their team as a whole. Developing great trust-filled relationships is a one-on-one event, not a one on many. Totaling a lump sum of the quality of your relationship with an entire team is the easy way out. The best way to do this is by focusing on each person on the team and sharing what I call the Trust Compound Theory.

The Trust Compound Theory

Each day you get the opportunity to build stronger bonds of mutual trust with your team by sharing your competence, showing you care, and exposing your character. Each member of your team is evaluating how much they trust you based on how well you do these three things (Figure 4.1).

FIGURE 4.1 Trust Is Built on Competence, Care, and Character

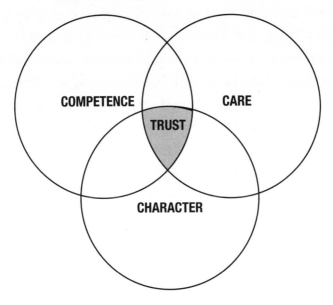

Competence

Competence hinges on the depth of your knowledge and how willing you are to impart that to others.

To the naked eye, Jim Estill was a fourth-year engineering student at University in Waterloo. Looking closer you could see his entrepreneurial spirit was ignited. Jim started a small company that bought, sold, and fixed computer parts. What separated him from the masses was his thirst for education around computers. Day in and day out he would study how computers were built, where the industry was going, and how to fix them when they were broken. Before long he became the go-to point of contact for students at the university. If there was a computer needing to be fixed or purchased, Jim was your man.

As Estill's small start-up business took off, he was forced to hire employees to help him keep up with the demand. He used the same model with his employees as he did for himself. He shared his vast technical competence about the business, the products it bought and sold, and the computer hardware industry as whole with each employee so they could then impart this knowledge on to customers. He didn't stop there, however. He also was fanatical about sharing his leadership skills with them as well because he know people with only technical competence can only go so far. With this, Jim's small side hustle grew to epic proportions because he scaled himself. Some 25 years later, the company started by one truly competent college student had grown to $350 million in annual sales and was purchased by SYNNEX.

The key to sharing your own competence is imparting the technical knowledge you have gained to those you lead as well as your leadership skills on an ongoing basis. Your willingness to share these two things is your ticket to building bonds that lead to big things. I will cover much more about the best ways to share competence in Chapter 10.

Care

In order for your team to understand how much you care about them, you must reject the notion that words hold great power. Instead, accept the power of actions.

In 2017, the Los Angeles Rams broke conventional wisdom and hired Sean McVay to be their new head football coach. He instantly became the youngest coach in the NFL at just 30 years old. McVay had a lot to prove, and he faced a challenging environment filled with people who had been in and on the field for much longer than him.

In a sport where age and experience creates a perception of one's ability, McVay rose to the challenge and showed that age was just a number. In his first two seasons his Los Angeles Rams went an impressive 24-8, won two Conference Championships, and earned an invitation to Super Bowl LIII, and he was named AP's NFL Coach of the Year. While McVay has the work ethic of many of the greats with the intellect to match, it's the care he has for his players and coaches that sets him apart. He explained this very well to his quarterbacks during a team meeting, saying, "One of the things that is consistent amongst all great leaders is they're a great teammate that is invested in the guys around them to raise the level of play. You do that by believing in guys and caring about them. When you care about the players you are working with, that's when they want to play hard for you."

In order to show your people you care as Sean McVay does, you have to get to know them on a professional and personal level. This starts with asking them questions about their own journey, experiences, challenges, and what drives them. Instead of just going through the motions, you have to be intent on listening and remembering so you can adjust your actions in the future to show them you listened.

Like all great relationships, the only way to get there is by dedicating time. A mentor of mine always told me, "Kids spell love T-I-M-E." The same is true in showing people you truly care about them. Your time is valuable, and you can't get it back. Devoting time to someone else shows that you care, and they are more important than anything else you have going on.

Another powerful way to show you care is to be vulnerable; share truths and ask for help when you need it. During an interview on the *How I Built This* podcast, Howard Schultz, founder of Starbucks Coffee, said, "The most undervalued characteristic of leadership is vulnerability and asking for help." A man who built a multibillion-dollar company from a small coffee bean shop places the ultimate emphasis on vulnerability. Regardless of his immeasurable success, Schultz has maintained the importance of sharing the truth with people in order to show them he cares about them as human beings.

The whole idea of vulnerability makes some people feel uncomfortable. The best and easiest way for any leader to practice it comes from a lesson I learned from Laszlo Bock, the former SVP of People at Google and current CEO of Humu. It consists of sending a short e-mail to your people that includes the following questions:

1. Tell me *one thing* you want me to *start* doing.
2. Tell me *one thing* you want me to *stop* doing.

This simple act of e-mailing your people with a genuine interest to get better at your job is a powerful act of vulnerability. It shows them you care about their opinion. Not only will it make you a better leader, but it will build stronger bonds with your team.

Character

General Caslen used to tell people at every board meeting, and in interactions all over the campus of West Point, "When you fail at character, you fail at leadership." Character is defined as the mental and moral qualities distinctive to you as an individual. It's an engraved set of disciplined habits and a settled disposition to do good. When there is clearly a right or wrong, the choice you make is based on your character. In the workplace, a person's character is put to the test frequently. These types of decisions are constant. If you stay in a leadership role long enough, you will be faced with many crucible moments where your own character will be tested. If you have been leading other people for very long, they already know the kind of character you possess. Conversely, if you are new to leading a team, those team members are going to be constantly looking out for ways in which you show your character. The simplest examples in which your team will evaluate your character includes things like:

- How do you treat others who have nothing to give you in return?
- How do you act in groups?
- Do you interrupt others when they are talking?
- What do you value most out of life?

There are many leaders who fail in their job. While there are many reasons for failure, a compelling argument can be made it's because leaders don't put enough time and effort into building quality trust-filled relationships with the people they are supposed to lead. The best part of building quality relationships is that it knows no age or experience. Trust-filled relationships can be developed by every leader, and if you don't have them everything else you try and do will be a major uphill battle.

CHAPTER SUMMARY

- Principle 2: Without strong relationships, you can't lead.
- Trust = Consistency + Time.
- Each and every day you get the opportunity to build stronger bonds of mutual trust with your team by sharing your competence, showing you care, and exposing your character.
- If you want trust-filled relationships, don't just look for commonalities.
- Your willingness to share your competence will build stronger bonds and lead to big things.

5

ENCOURAGE THE CULTURE

"If you are falling short in anything,
be ruthless with your environment."
—FATHER MIKE SCHMITZ

Principle 3: Culture Starts with You, But Your People Prove It

More than once, *Golf* magazine ranked Pine Valley Golf Club the number one course in the United States and on the globe. Most golfers won't ever get a chance to play the renowned course, let alone dream of having access to it regularly. As the son of the president of the Pine Valley Golf Club, Chip Brewer considered himself pretty lucky to have that privilege, and growing up, he immersed himself in the game of golf.

Despite an excellent track record, the pressure of living up to the legacy of his father, a two-time USGA Senior Amateur, constantly lingered. After playing college golf at the College of William and Mary and graduating, Chip made the decision to refocus his efforts on his business skills instead of his golf skills. His professional journey eventually led him to get his MBA at the Harvard Business School, and in 1991 he took a job working in the paper industry. Inevitably, his worlds soon meshed as a round of golf with an old friend led to a promising business introduction. This on-course connection with the CEO of Adams Golf led to a position with the company in 1998. He thrived immediately by pouring in his passion for the game and combining it with his great business education. Four years later in 2002, Chip climbed the ranks to become the CEO. After an incredible 10-year run with the upstart golf equipment manufacturer an executive search firm took notice, hiring him away to be the president and CEO of a struggling company named Callaway Golf.

From his extensive experience, Brewer knew there was a major challenge not only to his new company but to the entire industry. Once a favorite American pastime, golf was in decline as people moved away from their grandfather's game to shorter, less expensive entertainment options. If this wasn't a big enough problem for a new CEO, he soon realized many of Callaway's employees weren't giving the best they had to offer in terms of their thinking and behaviors every day.

Discouraging moments were plentiful in his early days at Callaway Golf; he knew he had to ignite his people in order to ignite his company but wasn't sure exactly how. His moment of clarity came with the development of a new golf club in 2013. His team brought Chip the product; they were excited about its finished form, but all he could see was how much it still needed to be improved.

He spoke to his team from the heart: "Our founder Ely Callaway created this company to make products that were demonstratively superior and pleasingly different. This product doesn't live up to that vision. Each and every one of you are talented professionals, and I just want you to make products you are proud of. I do not care how we have to do it and how many things we have to fail on—we aren't going to launch this product to the market because it isn't worthy of this organization."

The team stood in silence, dumbfounded. Moments passed before the responses finally came. Instead of excuses or rebuttals, they offered a consistent agreement. It was almost if they were relieved their new CEO was a leader who wasn't going to settle for average. From that point on, the change was palpable. Employees began staying late to work together, collaboration between departments became the norm, and new ideas were plentiful.

Chip knew that it was his job to encourage his people to explore and discover the answers while creating a culture that allowed them to their best work. In the golf business, this meant allowing team members the freedom to be creative and try innovative things. Thinking of new technology, building it, and then testing it can cost millions of dollars, and the majority of ideas or products fail more often than they become successful.

A revised version of the product was eventually presented to Chip, branded X Hot. This would end up being a transformational product in the golf industry that year, and it marked the beginning of Callaway's climb back to the top. While there are many reasons why the Callaway Golf team was able to be successful, it began with the environment and culture in which they worked.

Since 2013, Callaway Golf has produced an endless string of products that equal or surpass the success of the X Hot three-wood. Chip makes it a priority to literally and figuratively wrap his arms around people by championing their work and supporting both their success and failures. When I had the chance to sit down with him, Chip told me, "You cannot lose confidence in your people, and I love the people here. I choose that word *love* intentionally because I do not just like the people here or the environment we have created, I love it."

Callaway Golf has gone from a struggling golf brand in 2012 to the second-largest golf equipment company in the world and one of the few growing in a shrinking golf market. To give you an idea of the difficulty in the industry, most reports show golf sales shrinking between 1 and 3 percent year over year. One of Callaway's competitors, TaylorMade, was sold by its parent company Adidas after going from $1.7 billion in revenue in 2012 to around $900 million in 2016.

Conversely, Callaway's trend is moving in the opposite direction. The 2017 year produced net sales over $1 billion, a 20 percent increase over 2016. In 2018, improvement is even higher at 30 percent, leading Callaway Golf toward becoming the best golf brand in the world. Like all great leaders who focus on building the best, Chip gives credit where it is due. In a second-quarter 2018 public earnings call, he said, "I'd like to take this chance and thank the Callaway Golf team for delivering these results. The team should be proud of what we have accomplished. I'm also sure they understand we have a lot more to do and like me are motivated to take our company to the next level." Creating and maintaining an encouraging culture is difficult, but ultimately attainable. You may not be in the position to completely revamp your company culture.

A shift in companywide culture must start at the ground level with just the team in which you lead because culture comes to life at the team level first. But before you can mimic what Chip did at Callaway, you must understand what "culture" really means. "Culture" comes from the Latin word, *colere*, meaning, "to cultivate." I define culture in the modern business sense as the shared beliefs and values that guide thinking and behavior.

An easy way to test the strength of the shared beliefs and values on your team is to ask yourself: "If I were gone for a month, would the team carry on with their best thinking and behavior, or would they begin to slip?" Your answer will give you a hint about the current state of your team culture. If you are going to build the best, it is your job to ensure your culture promotes effective thinking and positive behavior of your people regardless of the circumstances.

Four elements make up any team's culture:

- **Safety.** Before people can perform at their best, they first need to feel safe and protected. How does the current environment make your people feel? First, are the working conditions physically safe? Second, do team members feel emotionally safe to share ideas and feelings without fear of any repercussions?
- **Unity.** Inclusivity and people feeling like they are part of something bigger than themselves help feed productivity and innovation. Does each person on your team feel like he or she plays an integral part? Does everyone work together as a team, or do they create silos or cliques? At the center of unity is mutual respect among team members and a feeling of belonging.
- **Positivity.** Beliefs drive people's actions, and actions drive results. If your team's beliefs are optimistic, the chances of good things happening in the future are drastically higher than the alternative.

Positivity is driven from the top down, and it's contagious.

- **Energy.** Energy keeps your team going and impacts the intensity and speed at which people perform. High energy yields high performance. You can always tell the energy of a team by what they're doing midday. Have they settled into complacency, or are they revving their engines to power through the rest of the day?

The level at which these elements are present determines the quality of your team's culture. You cannot have a successful culture if one or any of these elements aren't being fulfilled. The graphics in Figures 5.1 and 5.2 give an example of an elite team culture versus one that isn't.

FIGURE 5.1 Elite Team Culture

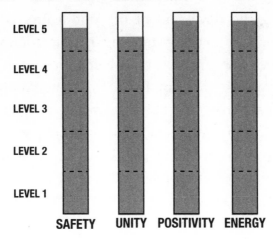

FIGURE 5.2 Deficient Team Culture

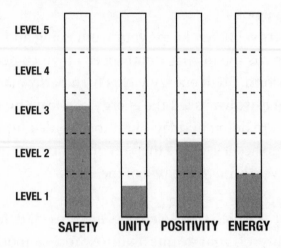

When all four of these elements are achieved simultaneously, at high levels, it's called an elite team culture. When the average of the four elements is at a level two, it's called a deficient team culture.

Leaving the development of your team's culture to chance will lead to things moving in a direction you may not like because the culture is being shaped every day whether you like it or not. If you do not mold and guide it, your team may end up disengaged, voluntary turnover will increase, and a lackluster attitude will develop. Conversely, your proactivity will give way to a more productive team, better morale, and overall positive results. Here is what you can do to actively increase each of the four elements of your team's culture.

Safety First

If you walked into a restaurant and the hostess asked whether you would like a booth or table in the open, how would you answer?

Most patrons would prefer to sit in a booth, and the reason why is subconscious. When sitting in a booth, you inevitably feel safer and protected. Human beings have a constant desire to feel safe, so that's where we naturally gravitate toward.

The need for safety extends to every facet of our lives including the workplace, specifically two key areas: physical and emotional safety.

Creating a physically safe environment is cut and dried. At a desk job, this is not typically an issue to address, but it may pose an issue if your team is in manufacturing or on a construction site. There are industry standards and rules in place that tell you, at a minimum, what to do to keep the environment physically safe. Letting your people know you're abiding by these rules and asking if there's anything you missed is always a good practice.

What isn't so cut-and-dried is creating an emotionally safe environment so people on a team are able to set aside their self-doubt, uncertainty, and fear so they can perform at their best. Turns out this is one of the most important things you can do as a leader to build the best and improve the culture. Google's Abeer Dubey, director of people analytics (HR), and Julia Rozovsky, a people analytics manager, led a two-year study called Project Aristotle, which evaluated 180 Google teams, conducted 200-plus interviews, and analyzed more than 250 different team attributes. Rozovsky outlined the five key characteristics of enhanced teams they found: dependability, structure and clarity, meaning, impact, and psychological safety. As interesting as all five of them are, the most important was psychological safety.

The only way for you to encourage a psychologically safe environment is by understanding that it starts with you. Specifically, your ability to create a collaborative environment that challenges the voices in your team's heads that provide doubt. You have to be intentional about creating an inviting workspace where people can share ideas, ask questions, and collaborate. If your team perceives their comments are going to be judged or not respected, they will begin to reserve those ideas and questions for a different environment altogether. There is a famous leadership quote from Andy Stanley that provides the key for you to create a safe environment: "Leaders who refuse to listen will eventually be surrounded by people with nothing helpful to say." A mentor of mine told me, hearing is through the ears but listening is through the mind. You have to make the choice to listen to the ideas and perspectives of others instead of just hearing them. Most people aren't good listeners because when they hear something they begin thinking about how they are going to respond. They begin formulating their points one by one, and the whole time the other person is still talking. Because listening is critical to creating psychological safety, I want to give you a few tips to help you develop the skill.

1. **Anchor yourself.** You can't listen until you are anchored into a conversation. Put away your phone or any possible distraction in order to anchor yourself. If for some reason you can't anchor because of other priorities, be honest and tell your team member you need to come back to this when you can anchor yourself.

2. **Consider what other are saying.** There is too much going on and too many variables for one leader to know it all. Ensure that when others are providing ideas or alternative ways of doing something you are truly considering what they are saying.

3. **Prove you listened.** The best way to create a psychologically safe environment is to prove to others you were listening by implementing what was said. While the implementation of every idea isn't possible, testing the idea or discussing it in more detail rather than disregarding it will be another sign to prove you listened.

A Unified Team

Everyone has a series of fundamental needs. One of these is the longing to belong and be connected to others. The psychological theory called "the need to belong" proposes people's sense of social belonging is indeed fundamentally required. Research conducted by Julianne Holt-Lunstad, Timothy B. Smith, and J. Bradley Layton in 2010 found the quality and quantity of social relationships is linked to mental health, morbidity, and mortality. Solid connections are as important to your health and happiness as food, water, and shelter.

In high school, I was named one of the captains of our football team. During one preseason, a new student named Jake transferred into our school and tried out for the team. He quickly became one of our better players. The only problem was that Jake never seemed to find unity with the other players.

After several weeks of Jake putting in the maximum effort during practice, he started to miss days and slack off during drills. I took notice and made my best effort to find out what was going on, but Jake was reluctant to talk. Just one week before our first game, the coach made an announcement. Jake would no longer be a part of our team; he had decided to quit. While most of my peers were unfazed by the news, it ate at me. Jake was a great asset to the team and could have helped us achieve big things.

Years later, I ran into Jake. I could not help but ask him why he made the decision to leave the team. He told me, "I just never felt like I belonged." It was clear at that moment, our team had failed him. We did not welcome him. Quite frankly, the opposite had occurred. Jake was excluded from gatherings after practice, and I know multiple times he had overheard negative comments from other players about the small town he had moved from. As team captain, I should have done more to make him feel an important part of the team.

It is a major responsibility as a leader to give your people this sense of belonging in order to create a unified team. Unity requires proactivity. There are many ways to go about it, but one of my favorite examples came from a leader I coached at a medium-size company; his name was Harry. He shared with me an incredible practice he uses to create a united team right after a new team member joins. Harry handwrites a note to each new hire, inviting them to be a part of the team. This formal note has become a big deal. Shortly after receiving the note, Harry has a one-on-one conversation with the recruit to truly invite the new member to be a part of the team from day one. This particular team does not suffer from silos, cliques, or having outsiders. The team, as he says, "works in harmony and together because people know they have been invited and their participation isn't a nice-to-have, it is warranted." The case can be made that this exercise shouldn't just be for new hires, but it could also be done for an entire team that isn't united in order to reset the human connections among the employees.

Effortless Positivity

Mike Erwin, a West Point graduate, served three tours of duty for his country. He transitioned out of the military in pursuit of a passion he discovered during his graduate studies at the University of Michigan.

Erwin explored the ins and outs of "positive psychology." This approach is that no matter how innately good or bad a person may seem, there are positive character traits present within everyone. He began writing about his work and shared it with friends and colleagues. His goal was for people to pull their best character traits out of themselves and others. Through what he calls "divine intervention," two old friends who were high school principals decided they wanted to teach the concepts of "positive psychology" to students in schools in Massachusetts and asked Erwin to help.

What started as a small pet project turned into a nationwide movement called the Positivity Project. It began at a single institution in 2015 and has grown to over 200 schools in 14 states with no signs of slowing down. With the program in place, teachers observed a 24 percent increase in students' ability to recognize, articulate, and appreciate others' strengths. Not only that, but their ability to articulate their own strengths rose 39 percent along with a 22 percent increase in peer-to-peer relationships.

As impressive as these numbers are, it's what's behind them that is so important. Erwin was able to instill the importance of a positive outlook and the belief that good things happen to students and teachers alike.

Erwin told me in an interview, "Of all 24 character strengths, optimism and the idea of being a positive leader is so important. Because of the information age we all live in, people are more in tune with all the challenges and negativity in the world. It has made it hard to be more optimistic. So to be an optimistic leader who is relentlessly positive in the face of challenges is a true competitive advantage."

While positivity, as Erwin suggests, is a true competitive advantage, it's also unique in that it's a choice you make for yourself. And the benefit of being positive creates a magnetic pull for like-minded people. Kim Cameron, associate dean of education at the Ross School of Business at the University of Michigan, cites the heliotropic effect in a 2018 TED Talk as to why this is the case. He said, "All living systems are inclined toward that which is life-giving and . . . avoid that which is life depleting," or "toward positive energy and away from negative energy." For example, "if you put a plant in the window, over time it leans toward the light."

Gravitating toward things that create vibrancy or are life-giving is in our human DNA. But as easy as it is to write about this, the world we live in is more complex than photosynthesis. You know what it feels like to be frustrated, disappointed, or to catch a bad break. For most people, it feels easier to adopt a negative point of view for the sake of saving face rather than looking for the positive in every situation.

If you want to have a culture that is encouraging for others, it is your responsibility to make a conscious effort to be positive. Take the heliotropic effect to heart and do everything in your power to be positive every day and in every situation. But for positivity to take root in your culture, it has to reach every individual on your team. The strategies are endless, but those leaders who are relentless about building the best leverage these strategies:

1. **When bad things happen, respond with a positive comment.** There is no doubt you'll experience frustration and events will happen that aren't

positive. In these moments ask yourself, "What is one possible positive outcome?" Regardless of how bad things might be on the surface, there is always a sliver of positivity that can shine through if you just adjust your perspective.

2. **Promote and encourage things that help create positive energy.** While work can and absolutely should be a place that helps create positive energy for people, it is easy to lose sight during difficult times. Find ways to promote other areas of life that typically create positive energy like going to church, healthy eating, physical fitness, and building quality personal relationships. This could mean a free gym membership for your team, healthy snacks around the office, or a paid vacation that allows team members to take their spouses away for a weekend.

3. **Remove the people that cause negativity.** Regardless of how good a performer someone is on your team, people's value must also be measured by the positivity they bring to the team. There's a famous saying, "Don't let one bad apple spoil the bunch." Each person, regardless of his or her role, plays a part in the ongoing development of your culture. One drop of negativity will spread like a cancerous cell. Consider what behavior you allow while continuing to promote positivity.

Contagious Energy

The last element of an encouraging culture is energy. Traditional thinking says energy comes from results. While this isn't wrong, energy can be produced, well before results are achieved, through the power of words or mantras.

In 2012, P.J. Fleck was hired by Western Michigan University as its head football coach. He was the youngest in the country at just 32 years old. At the time, there wasn't much excitement around the program. Fleck's first order of business was to implement activities that would add excitement. He introduced a program-wide mantra, "Row the Boat." This was designed to motivate players during times of difficulty, helping them remember not to give up. There were three parts: The oar stood for energy each person brings to the team. The boat was the sacrifice each member of the team had to make. And finally, the compass was what directed each team member down the path of success.

Fleck personally committed to this idea when his young son passed away. Although it was difficult, Fleck wanted to continue living his life as a tribute to his son's legacy. As the mantra caught on, energy in the program skyrocketed. However, the results did not translate at first. The team's first season was abysmal, compiling a win-loss record of 1-11. This did not discourage Coach Fleck, however. He stayed faithful, making it a priority to create an encouraging culture on and off the field. As a result, the following two seasons saw much improvement.

Everything seemed to come together in the 2016 season as Western Michigan went a perfect 13-0 in the regular season. They nabbed their first Mid-American Conference title since 1988. While they narrowly lost the Cotton Bowl, their newfound success catapulted Fleck into contention for the best young coach in college football. In 2017, he was rewarded with the head coaching position at the University of Minnesota.

Mantras are not specific to sports. Todd Weiden, a VP in the banking industry, was tasked with taking over one of the lowest-performing divisions in his company. It included more than 140 separate branches in Atlanta. Facing a division riddled with underwhelming performers and high turnover rates, Todd knew the only way he could turn the situation around was by building an elite culture. This would make it effortless for individuals to lean in and win. He began by setting incredibly high standards coupled with the mantra, "Run this town." These words influenced the team so positively they began to understand where they were missing the mark and self-corrected their behaviors. Over time, the teamwide initiative and proactivity were so prevalent that the vast majority of 140 branches were blowing the results out of the water as people strived to "run this town" again. Todd's people had a new sense of swagger and energy that abolished the old mentality with ease.

Imagine being a player on P.J. Fleck's team or team member of Todd Weiden's. Feel that jolt of energy? Run with it! Employ that energy you are imagining and pour it into your own people. Fleck's "Row the boat" and

Weiden's "Run this town" are just two examples of what I call a Maximizing Mantra; they are critical to energizing any team or company. A few of my favorite examples include:

- Let's Go
- Take Dead Aim
- Move the Needle

Part of your job as a leader is to ensure you have a Maximizing Mantra for your team, company, or even your family so you can create a similar sense of energy for others.

While this comes easier for some, I have seen it done well in various ways. One leader I coach struggled to come up with a Maximizing Mantra on her own, so she explained the concept in a team meeting. Within just a few minutes the entire group got behind one of the suggestions, "All Serve Customers." This fits perfectly in their industry selling commodity steel products. One of their only differentiators is how every employee serves their customers. Other leaders I have worked with look for inspiration from earlier in their life or from the hobbies they engage with outside of work.

Regardless of the method you use to get there, it's important that your Maximizing Mantra is simple, provides clarity, is action-oriented, and most importantly, is fun. Once you have one, put it on walls, on T-shirts, or in e-mails. Use it all the time and keep it in the forefront of your people's eyes and hearts.

When you put all of this together and you have a safe, unified, positive, and energized culture, keep it growing and evolving by providing recognition and praise to those best living out these things every day. This can come in the form of an award, gifts, or simply verbalizing it to people in person. The key when giving out praise and recognition is to be sincere and emphasize things that are under someone's control, things like attitude, effort, and actions.

CHAPTER SUMMARY

- Principle 3: Culture starts with you, but your people prove it.
- Culture is defined as the shared values and beliefs that guide thinking and behavior.
- Team cultures are molded each day whether leaders like it or not.
- The four elements of team culture are safety, unity, positivity, and energy.
- Being united with others can be as important as food, drink, and shelter.

6

CLARIFY THE PURPOSE

*"Activity without purpose is
the drain of your life."*
—TONY ROBBINS

Principle 4: People Persevere Because of Purpose Not Pay

The path was not always clear. In fact, it was foggy at best. Joanne Tate had recognized her love for education, but there was more to it. When Father "Smokey" Oats offered her the position of dean of students at a brand-new private school, she naturally resisted. Open a mere six months, there were just 103 students in attendance at Trinity Episcopal School. On her first visit, Joanne passed by the school twice missing the sign. A collection of trailers that served as the physical school buildings were a far cry from what she had envisioned. Everything seemed to be working against a move to Trinity. The pay was not great, and the position was unlike any she had held before. But as she thought and prayed over the decision, she felt a great joy about taking a job that pushed her well outside her comfort zone. So, she made the call to Father Oats and accepted.

On her first day in February 2003, Joanne arrived expecting a grandiose onboarding process. She was greeted with quite the opposite. She was led to a temporary trailer on the backside of the property and given a desk so small she could touch elbows with her two brand-new colleagues.

But it was what came next that reinforced her decision to start work at Trinity. Father Oats entered the room and with a warm welcome he clearly communicated what Joanne now calls the "Trinity Way." "Joanne, we are excited to have you as a part of the team. This school was born out of a vision from great community leaders to create an Episcopal school to serve the children of Charlotte, diverse, academically renowned, community-focused, Kingdom values–laden, and graduates who are making a positive difference in the world." He continued, "It's people like you and the other employees in this school who will bring this to life in conjunction with our faith in God, our board members, parents, and, most importantly, our students. We will always keep our mission of bringing the Episcopal tradition in both its unity and diversity and bringing the best experience we can to our students at the forefront of everything we do."

As Father Oats exited, Joanne could not help but feel immediately connected to her new surroundings and colleagues. She had not even officially begun her work, yet she knew her presence would matter.

The workdays flew by as Joanne hurled herself into learning, growing, and proactively helping Trinity best exemplify its mission. The "Trinity Way" that Father Oats had so poignantly communicated on her first day was not a one-time occurrence. Faculty talked about it and reinforced it day in and day out. The mission, vision, and core values became ingrained in Joanne and her colleagues. It not only guided the staff's hiring, firing, budgeting, and enrollment decisions, but it shaped the decision making of teachers, students, parents, and funders.

Joanne had never been a part of a group that was singing from the same hymn sheet like this. While it did not come without challenges, everyone was able to build up the success of Trinity based on their clear understanding of its purpose. Because of this, word spread quickly in town about what this faith-based school was doing to create a diverse and exceptional academic experience. Student growth accelerated quickly; by the school's second year the student population had more than doubled in size and included 233 students. What was once a far-out vision in the eyes of a few had become a reality for the community. Father Oats, Joanne, the entirety of Trinity Episcopal staff, and students knew from the very inception what made up their mission, vision, and values. To this day, those things are still a part of the school's very DNA.

Words like *excellence, strength, community, distinction,* and *commitment* are not just buzzwords. They are the keys to attracting talented teachers, building great curriculum, having a diverse student population, and communicating a unified message. While the "Trinity Way" is unique to Trinity Episcopal School, no one has a patent on being purpose-driven. Each leader not only has the ability to connect his or her team to being purpose-driven, but it's also a requirement in today's modern times. With so many options for people to choose from when it comes to where they work or what team they join, those leaders who are intensely connected to their purpose stand out from the crowd. It also fuels a team to continue to pursue their purpose when times are difficult or challenging.

Unfortunately, many leaders aren't interested in being purpose-driven because it feels soft. The most common comment I get is, "This purpose stuff is fluffy. We are here to make money." Others flat out say, "We just don't need it." While I can absolutely understand why people would say these things, they could not be more wrong.

There are many examples that show the value of being a purpose-driven leader, but none is better from a for-profit business standpoint than Chick-fil-A and its founder Truett Cathy.

For almost four decades from 1946 to the early 1980s, the company saw slow and consistent growth. So much so that Cathy finally felt comfortable to expand the corporate environment and made a big land purchase in the Atlanta area to build the company's headquarters. It was a major personal investment that stretched him and his company thin. About the same time, the company saw its first decline in sales. There was major concern among the employee base, who anticipated a major layoff because of the combination of the losses and new land investments.

One weekend during this particularly turbulent time, Cathy invited the entire management team on a weekend retreat. It was his goal to figure out how they were going to address their current hardships, which most people linked to branding, store locations, and an overall lack of marketing. But instead of focusing on these details, Cathy brought up something entirely different: purpose. For three days the group of leaders racked their brains and came up with Chick-fil-A's purpose statement: "To glorify God by being a faithful steward of all that has been entrusted to us. To have a positive influence on all those who come into contact with Chick-fil-A." Following the retreat, a companywide meeting was held, and instead of pink slips, as many employees feared, Cathy shared the work the management team had done over the weekend and clearly communicated the new purpose statement. He made it clear that any decision the company would make from that point forward would be in alignment with this purpose statement. He also challenged each team member to ensure their actions and behaviors every day made a positive influence on anyone who came into contact with Chick-fil-A. Following the meeting, the purpose statement was carved into a big stone outside of their new company headquarters and remains there to this day. Not only has it stood the test of time, but Truett's son, Dan Cathy, who currently leads the company, continues to hold the purpose statement at the forefront of everything the company does.

Here is the best part. Chick-fil-A has not seen another major decline in sales since the purpose statement was created and cemented into the fabric of the business. As impressive as the streak of growth is, the domination over the competition should tell you there is something to this purpose stuff. In 2017, Chick-fil-A earned more per store than any other fast-food restaurant. A lot more. In fact, the average revenue of a Chick-fil-A store was $4 million in 2017. That's more than a McDonald's, Starbucks, and Subway combined. If that wasn't enough, their nearest competitor in the chicken vertical, Kentucky Fried Chicken (KFC), averaged around $1.1 million of revenue per store. And, do not forget Chick-fil-A is only open six days per week while these competitors are open seven. It sounds crazy because it is.

How to Get Started

Three cornerstones are necessary to clarify a purpose, what I call the purpose trifecta. Its name comes from horse racing, where a bettor can make a wager on the outcome of a race through a trifecta bet. The bettor must have all three horses picked—who will finish first, second, and third in the correct order. If the horses do this, the bet yields a higher payout than any other form of wager in the sport.

The same is true for clarifying a purpose. The purpose trifecta is made up of values, vision, and mission (Figure 6.1). These tend to be evergreen and rarely falter. Clarifying these three parts will dramatically increase your odds building the best team and organization.

FIGURE 6.1 Purpose Trifecta

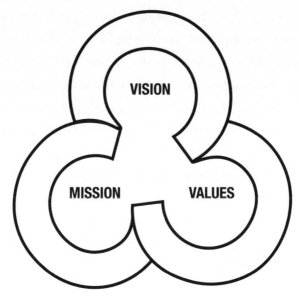

VISION

MISSION

VALUES

Values

Core values are the fundamental beliefs a person or team holds true. Once established, these guiding beliefs dictate behavior and help individuals decipher right from wrong.

A common denominator of all leaders who build the best is the time they dedicate to defining a set of core values. But they don't stop at defining the values. Instead, they make those values part of the team's guiding light. Values come alive not through words on a wall or a website but through the actions of everyone in the organization. Talented people are not attracted to empty words, but rather the exercising of them. Rewarding, recognizing, and talking about them on an ongoing basis provides a clear expression of how important they are to you and your people.

● ● ●

On January 11, 2014, Penn State University and its athletic department announced the hiring of football coach James Franklin. Franklin was recruited from Vanderbilt University after three of the most successful years in the football team's history. The opportunity was comparable to being promoted from the junior varsity to varsity team. To put it into perspective, Vanderbilt's football stadium has a 39,750 capacity while Penn State's Beaver Stadium has a capacity of 106,572. As the community was still healing from the Jerry Sandusky child abuse case in 2011, Franklin's new gig was not without challenge. While the storied program had two National Championships, the last one was in 1986.

Franklin wasted no time in his new leadership role. One of the first things he did was establish four core values for his team. They were simple, yet difficult to live out:

- Positive attitude
- Great work ethic
- Compete in everything you do
- Must be willing to sacrifice what the common man will not

His entire coaching staff and team members were measured against these four core values, and the values were plastered on walls, on shirts, and in team binders. Players and coaches could not go anywhere in the football facility without being reminded of them. Franklin knew it was not the words themselves that were important, but rather everyone living out the values.

To help make the success of the team a reality, Franklin knew he had to reward, recognize, and talk about these core values in a public setting. Each week during the football season, Franklin and his staff gathered the entire team and gave out an award to one player in front of the entire team. This award was not about the most valuable player from the previous week's game, but instead, the one who had best lived out the core values on the team and in the community. In just a few short weeks, behavior on the team changed. Players, hungry for the recognition and respect of their peers, wanted to win the award. They made choices to live out the core values both in and outside of their football duties.

Imagine how much more successful a football team is going to be on the field when 120 people are choosing to have a positive attitude and great work ethic. Franklin's players did just that, and the results multiplied tenfold. In the five seasons since Franklin took over, the team achieved a record of 45-21, attended five bowl games, won the Big Ten title, and entered back in the discussion as one of the premier football programs in the country.

I cannot stress enough that core values by themselves do absolutely nothing. If Coach Franklin defined those four core values, put them on walls and on shirts, but never rewarded, recognized, or talked about them, they would not have changed anyone's behavior. Worse, if he personally didn't live them out himself, his words would be meaningless and easy to disregard. The power in core values is the exercising of them on an everyday basis—by everyone.

You have the ability to do the same thing Franklin did for your organization, team, or even your family. If you have never sat down and defined the core values of your team or organization, don't wait another day. If you don't know where to start, take this list of common core values and narrow it down to four or five that best align to the group you lead:

- Hard work
- Work ethic
- Loyalty
- Honesty
- Consistency
- Serving

- Creativity
- Courage
- Perseverance
- Ownership
- Humor
- Open-mindedness
- Reliability
- Compassion
- Competitiveness
- Will
- Passion
- Empower

When you come up with a final list, design a phrase that brings it to life. Skookum Digital Design, a software development and design company based in Charlotte, North Carolina, provides an incredible example of this. The business began growing rapidly as the need for custom software solutions grew in enterprise organizations all over the country. The management team needed a way to make sure that as the team grew and they weren't able to be involved in all of the hiring decisions and day-to-day activities, the organization knew what values it cared deeply about. Instead of creating core values from scratch, they codified them for future employees from things that were already being lived out. The team defined four core values and later added one more:

- Simplify and Go
- Embrace Change

- Own It
- Choose to Be Happy
- Give More Than You Take

To ensure the values became ingrained in the organization for the long haul as part of the company's interview process, all potential employee complete a Skookum Core Values interview. During the interview, each prospective employee is introduced to the core values and the meaning behind each one, and it's clearly described to them that Skookum hires and fires based on these values. Finally, interviewees are asked questions to demonstrate their alignment to the values and asked to withdraw from consideration if they believe they aren't aligned with them.

As effective as this process is, the business has experienced employees who didn't end up agreeing with the values or slipped through the cracks during the interview process. The leaders in the organization have not hesitated to part ways with these people. While terminating employees is never a fun thing to do, the colleagues of the employees who had to be let go end up appreciating the business for taking action because it strengthens their belief and understanding of the five core values.

It doesn't stop there. Skookum employees live out these values by giving their time and energy to make the people around them better, especially their clients. Every client is given an overview of the values. Part of the company living out those values means they work themselves out of a job by preparing their clients to take over the efforts and products completed by the team over time.

As the values have become more ingrained, the management team has created a "People Team" that is tasked with looking for creative ways to reward and recognize the team members who best live out these values every day, month, quarter, and year.

The Skookum core values, much like James Franklin's values at Penn State, have had a lot of thought and work put into them. Put in the work for your company or team to ensure you have defined values that go beyond words and best exemplify the fundamental beliefs you hold true.

Vision

Think back to the definition of leadership: inspiring, empowering, and serving in order to elevate others over an extended period of time. What I want to emphasize is "over an extended period of time." It is extremely difficult to create an improved state for a long time without first delivering a vision of a vastly better future.

The best leaders are visionaries. They have in view what is possible in the future. The late great Dr. Myles Munroe used to say, "Vision is the capacity to see beyond what your eyes can see." This may sound funny, but your eyes are actually the enemy in regard to you becoming a better visionary leader. This is because they are limited to what you can physically take in.

In 1961, President John F. Kennedy was visiting NASA headquarters for the first time. While touring the facility, he introduced himself to a janitor who was mopping the floor and asked him what he did at NASA. The janitor replied, "I'm helping put a man on the moon!"

The janitor got it. He understood NASA's vision and his part in it even though most others would say he was just mopping the floors.

Christopher Wren, the great English architect, is another great example. He was surveying St. Paul's Cathedral in London while it was under construction. When he came upon a workman, he asked a simple question, "What are you doing?" The man replied, "I am cutting a piece of stone." As he continued walking around the huge building, he posed the same question to another worker, and the man replied, "I am earning five shillings, two pence a day." He continued walking and asked a third worker the same question and the man answered, "I am helping Sir Christopher Wren build a beautiful cathedral." That man understood the vision. He could see beyond the cutting of the stone, beyond the earning of his daily wage, to the creation of a work of art—the great cathedral.

In modern times, there is no better example of a visionary leader than Elon Musk, founder of PayPal, Tesla, and SpaceX. While astronauts have ventured into space for decades, Musk and his team at SpaceX are fervently working on space travel for the citizen population. Musk set out a beautiful and bold vision for his team, "We are going to land people on Mars by 2025." Imagine coming to work every single day working to put human beings on Mars!

You don't have to be the president of the United States, a famous architect, or a tech titan to have a vision people can get behind. While it is true some people may have an easier time thinking in a future tense, every single person can close their eyes and see beyond what is right in front of them.

Ask yourself these questions about the future: "What does it look like? What is happening on the team or in the company? How many people are joining you on the journey? What kinds of people? What is the celebration going to look like? How are you going to feel? How is your team going to react? What is your family going to say? How will the world be different? How will the lives of the people you touch in the process be different?"

You are likely curious about how you go about creating a vision statement. While there is not an exact science to it, the trick is to find something that your team gets excited about. Something that will leave others in disbelief when your team achieves it. Whether you have proactively thought about a vision for your team, organization, or family before, it's worth doing the following exercise. Find yourself a quiet place. Put on one of your favorite songs, close your eyes, and envision big, bold possibilities in the distance. Make it worthy of hearing people say, "No way, that is just not possible."

Mission

In my experience, there is no exact formula to dictate how an organization or team should lay out its mission statement. My favorite organizational examples include the following:

- **Chick-fil-A:** To glorify God by being a faithful steward of all that has been entrusted to us. To have a positive influence on all those who come into contact with Chick-fil-A.
- **Movement Mortgage:** We exist to love and value people by creating a Movement of Change in our Industry, Corporate Cultures, and Communities.
- **Trinity Episcopal School:** Committed to the breadth of the Episcopal tradition in both its unity and diversity and bringing the best experience we can to our students.
- **LearnLoft:** We exist to turn professionals into leaders and create healthier places to work.

Many leaders struggle to determine their mission statement. What has always helped me and those I teach in our Building the Best workshops is to think about the mission in a military sense. No military operation is set in motion without a clear mission. For example, Seal Team Six, which killed Osama Bin Laden, was put in harm's way to carry out a specific mission: to take out the world's most dangerous man. While I don't believe there is a perfect formula to use, my friend Roderic Yapp, a former Royal Marines officer, shared a formula that I now share with others who struggle with defining their mission:

We do X in order to achieve Y for Z.

Broken down, it is simply what you do, why you do it, and for whom it is done. The key is to define your mission in a way that everyone can identify why decisions are made and actions are taken. The mission should always take precedence over how an individual may feel about a situation. With this mentality, a business, team, or family is always moving forward regardless of outside influencers.

Defining Mission on the Front Line

Creating a mission and vision statement along with defining core values might seem like something above your current role. In many organizations, the mission, vision, and values come from the executive team. While the purpose trifecta can absolutely be created within each individual team in a larger organization, there's a lighter version that can be just as impactful for a frontline manager of a team.

Take the example from an operations team working inside Movement Mortgage.

Casey Crawford and his management team had been working on empowering every team within the company to experiment and learn what their mission and purpose was in the context of the larger organization. One group was responsible for preparing final loan documents for the closing appointment for all parties to sign prior to the transfer of the deed. It's tedious and stressful work without a lot of real excitement. The team's manager saw an opportunity to create a deeper connection to the purpose behind the work her team was doing every day. She asked Movement loan officers who received the final documents from her team to send her pictures of Movement clients executing the final paperwork.

Soon after, a photograph of a single mother with her young daughter arrived. Both of them beamed with pride as the mother signed the paperwork solidifying the purchase of their very first home. Photographs like this one continued to roll in. As they did, this team within a large company like Movement Mortgage understood how instrumental they were in helping families become homeowners.

If you lead a team within a larger organization, do not go another minute without being clear on why your team does what it does and its purpose. It's easy for people to get lost in the monotony of their everyday work without even considering not only how their work impacts the organization but also how it impacts people beyond its walls. By creating a team mission statement to magnify the team's purpose, you immediately raise the ceiling of what's possible, and when things get difficult, the mission will give your team a reason to continue on, even through the most trying times.

A team's mission can follow the same formula as an organization's: We do X in order to achieve Y for Z.

For the Movement Mortgage team responsible for preparing final loan documents, the mission could be something like this: We rapidly compile and complete closing documents for families so they can be "home" as soon as possible.

Whether you have previously defined the purpose trifecta for your team or if this is the first you have thought about it, don't skip this important step. Leaders who are purpose-driven not only will be more successful in the long term versus those who aren't, but it's a requirement in today's leadership landscape.

CHAPTER SUMMARY

- Principle 4: People persevere because of purpose not pay.
- The purpose trifecta is made up of values, vision, and mission.
- The most important thing frontline managers can do is connect their specific team to the purpose of their work.
- Core values are the fundamental beliefs a person or team holds true.
- Put values into a phrase to make them come to life.
- Vision is the capacity to see beyond what the eyes can see.

PART III

BALANCE PEOPLE AND PERFORMANCE

7

EXECUTE
EVERY DAY

*"A good plan, violently executed now
is better than a perfect plan tomorrow."*
—GEORGE PATTON

Principle 5: Goals Aren't Achieved Without Priorities Put into Action

In 1983, a 21-year-old man got out of his dad's car to get on a train going to New York City for his first big interview with the Xerox company. Right before he stepped on the train he turned and said, "Dad, I guarantee you I'm coming home tonight with an employee badge in my pocket" His dad responded, "You're a good guy, Bill, but don't put all that pressure on yourself. Do the best you can."

On the train, Bill reviewed the Xerox annual report for the fifth time to ensure he was ready to talk about the company's current vision. It focused on the reinvention of Xerox and its new strategy called Total Quality Management. He convinced himself he could be a major catalyst in the reinvention of the company. But when he arrived at the hiring center, there were dozens of polished interviewees who appeared more experienced than he was.

A woman finally called his name. Before entering the room, he paused and thought about his humble beginnings growing up on Long Island and the excitement he had felt on the train reading that Xerox annual report. Refocused, he stepped into the interview room.

The next hour and a half was a blur. Bill spoke about his entrepreneurial background, his passion for the Xerox business, and how much he wanted to play a major part in the future vision at the company. As the interview was wrapping up, the hiring manager said, "Bill, it has been a great discussion. Thank you very much; the Human Resources department will be in touch with you in a couple of weeks." While most people would have been happy with the response, Bill wasn't satisfied. "I don't think you understand the situation, sir," Bill insisted. "I haven't broken a promise to my father in 21 years, and I guaranteed him that I was coming home from this interview with an employee badge in my pocket tonight." The hiring manager thought about it for a few seconds and said, "Bill, as long as you haven't committed any crimes, you're hired." As Bill walked out of the building riding a wave of energy, he found the nearest pay phone and called his dad. "Get out the champagne, I got the job."

Over the next nine years, Bill outperformed everyone else, knocking on doors for cold calls, selling copy machines and electronic typewriters. At the ripe age of 30, he got an offer to take on a leadership position running the Puerto Rico and Virgin Isles office for Xerox. Most people were excited for him, but some said it was a curse because the office was ranked 67 out of 67 in the company's sales rankings.

Bill went down to scout it out. Feeling good about the people and the opportunity, he made the decision to move his young family to Puerto Rico and take the promotion. For the first two weeks after taking the job, Bill did nothing but listen to the people and meet with the entire team one-on-one. He asked them questions like, "What is making us perform so poorly?" "What is really going on here?" and "Why are we dead last?"

After all the meetings, Bill determined the root cause of the team's poor performance. What the people wanted was leadership. They wanted a vision they could believe in; they wanted to be motivated to come to work again; and most importantly, they wanted to celebrate again (the last sales leader had cut expenses and eliminated the company Christmas party).

With their feedback in mind, Bill laid out a vision in a teamwide meeting. Making the vision a reality and driving the business forward would require an extreme level of professionalism and accountability. He promised his team, "Not only are we going to be great at what we do, but we are also going to be the #1 Xerox business in the entire world. We are going to go from #67 to #1!" At that moment, all the air left the room. The team immediately thought the goal was unachievable and pictured Bill on a plane back to New York City in just a few months.

Before the doubt and negativity spiraled out of control, he continued, "I have arranged for the return of our annual Christmas party. I have already booked the San Juan hotel and hired the #1 salsa singer in Puerto Rico. *When* we hit #1, we are going to celebrate like champions. To get there we are going to take it one day at a time, one week at a time, one month at a time, and one quarter at a time. I trust you and you trust me. We will work together to will this goal to happen." As Bill paused he looked over the room and saw a tiny spark in everyone's eyes.

It didn't take long to see the transformation begin. At the end the first quarter, Puerto Rico had improved a little in the Xerox stack rankings. The second quarter continued the momentum, and the team moved up even higher in the rankings. By the third quarter, they were on the cusp of achieving their goal. By the time the fourth quarter had come and gone, Puerto Rico had surpassed all the other teams to fill the number one spot at Xerox. Bill lived up to his end of the bargain and threw his team and their families the biggest party Puerto Rico had ever seen.

Bill McDermott has gone on to become the CEO of SAP, one of the largest software companies in the world. Bill figured out that in order for any team to execute at the highest level, it requires people to work on the right priorities and come together to will a dream to happen every day. No one is as smart, motivated, or passionate as a collection of people put together.

Bill's story isn't out of reach for anyone. He tied his goal to a system and was able to achieve it. In this chapter we are going to dig into a system you can leverage to achieve big (or small) things.

The GPI System

The person with a million good ideas loses to the entrepreneur who has one good idea and executes well. The football team that can execute the game plan and make the most plays wins. The sales team that executes their sales process to near perfection wins the big deals. The Marketing department that produces content that hits their prospective customers in the heart wins. Same goes in leading a team.

While your purpose trifecta of mission, vision, and values remains solid and steady over time, it must be put into action. In order to do that, it has to be broken down further into an actionable system everyone on your team can buy into and use as a grounding force as they take ownership of their daily decisions. It's what I call the GPI System: goals, priorities, and initiatives (Figure 7.1).

GPI puts the purpose trifecta into an actionable format that leaves nothing to question. It's the step-by-step directions your team will follow to get you from a short-term goal to a long-term vision.

FIGURE 7.1 The GPI System

Goals

David Schroeder had come to Quicken Loans Mortgage Services from a technology start-up to bring entrepreneurial ideas to a business that sorely needed it. It didn't take long for the six-foot-five-inch man with perfect hair to build great relationships and make a positive impact. With Schroeder at the helm, the group soared to new heights of achievement and was recognized as one of the best places to work in their region.

One of Schroeder's responsibilities was managing an internal technology and development team. The team had done incredible work over Schroeder's tenure, but they were falling behind on a big software development project that was critical to the rest of the company's success.

Schroeder set a short-term goal to complete the project prior to a big all-hands meeting in Las Vegas at the end of the year. He went to his development team and said, "If we finish this new software development project prior to the all-hands meeting, I will let you guys shave this beautiful head of hair in front of the entire company."

Putting his hair, which was never out of place, on the line created an immediate positive reaction from the team. He wrote in big letters on the team's whiteboard, "Project complete before Las Vegas = shave David's head." David and the team began by listing the major priorities that needed to be focused on in order to achieve the aggressive goal. Day in and day out the team focused their work efforts within the priorities and worked with an intensity Schroeder hadn't ever seen before. The team completed the major project on time, and at the all-hands meeting, everyone in the company roared with excitement as the team shaved David's glorious coiffure onstage.

What did the story of Bill McDermott during his time in Puerto Rico and David Schroeder at Quicken Loans

Mortgage Services have in common? They both used a formula to set a team goal that helped their team achieve more than they would have without it:

Clear Objective + Completion Date + Carrot

In McDermott's story, he had a clear objective: become the top-performing organization at Xerox + completion date: the end of the year + carrot: the biggest party Puerto Rico had ever seen.

In David's story, he had a clear objective: complete this technology project + completion date: by the all-hands meeting + carrot: the team could shave David's head in front of everyone.

The verb form of the word *team* means coming together as a group to achieve a common goal. Setting a clear goal for your team is instrumental in achieving your vision.

The team will be far more likely to succeed if the goal is specific and each member gets behind it. Research done by Dr. Gail Matthews found people are 42 percent more likely to achieve a goal if it's written down. The key after defining the goal and a completion date will be coming up with the "carrot" that helps motivate the team to achieve the goal. If this important step is missed, the likelihood each individual sustains the amount of work ethic required to achieve the goal every day is drastically lowered.

If you haven't already created a clear goal for your team, don't fret. Use the formula to come up with one.

Clear Objective + Completion Date + Carrot
= Your Team Goal

Your team goal should be revisited every year, or it can be leveraged to help accomplish a big objective on a shorter timeline. One of the most popular questions I get in the Building the Best workshops is, "Is it okay if my team goal is a revenue goal?" If you lead a team in the business world and revenue is how you as a leader are measured, it is completely acceptable for the goal to be a revenue or earnings number. However, if the team doesn't earn any additional compensation when they hit that number, then it shouldn't be the only goal. In that particular case, the achievement of the team goal would only benefit you and not the team. The key to your goal has to be something the team will get excited about achieving. Here are a couple of examples of things you can tie your goal to:

- Customers positively impacted
- Games won
- Industry award received
- Highest ranking team in the company
- Perfect execution
- Revenue or earnings
- Number of new customers won

I don't want to spend a lot of time on what you should do if the team goal can't be achieved because I know your team will make it happen. However, if you must know when you should disengage your team from a previously set goal, evaluate the following two components:

1. When the cost gets too high
2. When it takes too much time

Cost can mean many things. It can obviously be financial, but it can also be the ruining of personal relationships or your health or that of team members. Time, on the other hand, is one of the few things we can never get back. So if the amount of time required to achieve the goal is so great that it is taking away time from doing more important things, reevaluate the goal.

The leaders who build the best do an incredible job of setting both team and individual goals. They go through the same process for setting individual goals as they do with setting their team goals to help elevate the performance of each individual member of the team.

Priorities Accelerating Growth

If you've ever set a personal goal for yourself, you know setting the goal and achieving it are two very different things. Consider the last time you went on a diet. Let's say you started your diet with a goal to lose 20 pounds. Twenty pounds is the ultimate result you are trying to achieve. In order to achieve your goal of losing 20 pounds, you have to focus on three big areas: exercise, diet, and motivation. These are the things that, if you make them a top priority, will help you achieve your goal. If one or more of them are lacking, it becomes extremely difficult to know what to do each day, and ultimately, your odds of achieving your weight loss goal are slim (pun intended).

Regardless of your industry or the nature of the work your team does, you must have defined priorities if you want to hit your team goal. These are specific things that are regarded as more important than other things. The team at LearnLoft has a goal for the year: impact the lives of 10,000 leaders using the Building the Best Principles. In order for us to reach that goal, we identified five priorities for the entire team to focus on. These priorities are visible at each team meeting.

1. Developing the core Building the Best curriculum
2. Proactive marketing
3. Building sales pipeline
4. Fostering current client relationships
5. Delivering the Ultimate Leadership Academy

These priorities remain the same through the year, but their order of importance shifts, depending on the season of the business. This allows each member of our team to make their own decisions about their task lists as long as they remain within the five priorities.

Warning: it's easy to get caught in the "shiny penny" mode where everything you come across looks like a worthwhile pursuit. While exhilarating at the moment, a "shiny penny" detour puts goal achievement in danger. An old mentor always tells me you should be careful of the words you use in front of your team because "suggestions become orders."

A great example of the dangers of this came from a frontline manager in one of our workshops. He was surprised when he opened up his BTB Leader Report to find a common theme in the comments section under "What is one thing your leader could do to improve?" Every single response included the word *focus*. When asked, his peers shared examples of how his new ideas were quickly put into action by his team, while other, more important initiatives were abandoned. Instead of getting defensive, he had a moment of clarity. In front of his peers, he defined the five biggest priorities for his team and committed to sticking to them for the next six months in order to achieve a team goal he established in the workshop.

No one is immune to the temptations of a new idea or exciting project. To ensure you don't unintentionally veer off course, come up with the top priorities that will help achieve your big goal. These are things that I have come to call PAG, short for "priorities accelerating growth."

If you have never defined priorities consider specific areas within products, people, projects, or job functions. When evaluating your own priorities in these areas ask yourself, "Will focusing on this help our team achieve our goal?"

Here are some examples of priorities accelerating growth for leaders in different industries to get you started:

Vice President of Sales
1. Team skill development and knowledge acquisition
2. Aligning with marketing
3. CRM adoption
4. Sales process execution

Vice President of Accounting
1. Talent development
2. Technology enhancement

3. Accounts payable / accounts receivables

4. Serve internal and external customers

5. Reporting

Head Football Coach

1. Physical fitness

2. Team building

3. Dedicated and purposeful practice

4. Film study

5. Game plan design and study

FIGURE 7.2 Priorities Accelerating Growth

GOAL: Impact the lives of 10,000 leaders using the Building the Best principles

PRIORITIES ACCELERATING GROWTH

Develop Building the Best Core Curriculum

Proactive Marketing

Build the Sales Pipeline

Foster Current Client Relationships

Deliver the Ultimate Leadership Academy

Your PAG list (Figure 7.2) is an incredible place to focus if you've never defined priorities. Much like defining a goal, priorities by themselves don't do a whole lot. Your team must make decisions every day in alignment with those priorities in order for them to drive real results. That's why the GPI System goes one step deeper into initiatives.

Initiatives to Make Impact

An entrepreneur for over 20 years, Mac Lackey has built and sold five companies and raised more than $75 million in capital. Needless to say, he knows a thing or two about reaching a goal and leveraging priorities. In his first startup, he and his cofounder were working 70+ hours a week, doing everything they could to help the business grow and mowing through tasks. One day about six months into the start of the business, Lackey was sitting at his desk staring at his to-do list, and it hit him like a ton of bricks. He was exhausted, overwhelmed, and working on the wrong things. It was in that moment he thought back to a lesson a college professor had taught him called the Pareto principle. The principle states that if you spend your time working on tasks that rank in the top 20 percent of importance, you will see an 80 percent return on investment. As Lackey looked back at his to-do list, he could tell instantly which things would likely produce an 80 percent return on investments versus the others.

Lackey came up with a simple method that focuses on daily tasks that will "move the needle" for his company. Each day he pulls out a three-by-five notecard and writes WMN on the top. Underneath he fills out his to-do list with initiatives that will help his company "move the needle." He aptly calls his method WMN or "what moves the needle."

Lackey's WMN daily strategy is a fantastic way for you and your entire team to execute within your previously defined PAG list. Instead of thinking of this as a big change, just consider the fact that you and probably everyone on your team either writes down their initiatives each day or keeps a mental checklist. WMN ensures you aren't just making a to-do list full of tasks to check off, but instead working on things that will move the team or business forward (Figure 7.3). It's not about the number of things you get done, but rather the weight your work carries. Once you and your team get in the habit of completing daily initiatives in alignment with the PAG list, it will only be a matter of time for the positive results to follow.

FIGURE 7.3 Sample WMN List

WMN TODAY
Write a blog
Follow up on sales opportunity
Schedule podcast interview on empathy
Share social image on LinkedIn

Putting It All Together

The beautiful thing about the entire GPI System is that all three parts work together. Every leader, regardless of experience level or role in the organization, must make the team aware of a clear goal and get buy-in. If everyone is on the same page about the achievement of that particular goal, set up the priorities accelerating growth to ensure the team knows the things that are regarded as more important than another in order to reach that goal. Once everyone is clear on the priorities accelerating growth, team members can have the autonomy and ownership to take control of their daily initiatives to help the team be successful.

Communicating GPI to your team once or twice a year isn't enough. Add chief repetition officer to your title. Consistent communication is critical to ensure your team gets into the habit of using GPI as their grounding force.

CHAPTER SUMMARY

- Principle 5: Goals aren't achieved without priorities put into action.
- In order for any team to execute at the highest level, it requires people who come together to will a dream to happen every single day. No one is as smart, motivated, or passionate as a collection of people put together.
- Team Goal = Clear Objective + Completion Date + Carrot.
- Identify specific priorities in order to achieve the goal.
- Ensure the entire team is using a "what moves the needle" (WMN) to-do list aligned to the priorities.
- Be the chief repetition officer when it comes to the GPI System: goals, priorities, and initiatives.

8

ALIGN THE BEHAVIORS

"Leadership is the art of getting someone else to do something you want done because he wants to do it."
—DWIGHT D. EISENHOWER

Principle 6: The Instant You Lower Your Standards Is the Instant Performance Erodes

Certain companies tend to outperform their competition year after year. They sell similar products or services and are in similar locations, but for some reason or another, they keep crushing the competition.

Chick-fil-A is one of these companies that blows their competition out of the water. While their food is great, what really differentiates them isn't the food—it's how they make customers feel. The Chick-fil-A leadership pipeline comes alive every day through the actions and behaviors of employees who serve customers. What's amazing is the people who work in Chick-fil-A restaurants don't earn much more than industry standards.

Chick-fil-A leaders set high standards and work tirelessly to improve the performance of their people so every customer has a great experience. The most famous of all Chick-fil-A standards is how employees respond to customers after a simple "thank you." Every employee from the CEO to the person behind the register responds with, "It's my pleasure."

It started with their founder, Truett Cathy, and now flows through his son Dan and the entire staff across the country. As the story goes, Cathy was staying in a high-end hotel while on a business trip. Throughout the stay, the staff would respond to him with, "It's my pleasure to serve you." Cathy fell in love with the way this made him feel as a customer of the hotel. He wanted to create a similar experience within Chick-fil-A. When he got back to work on Monday he told the executive management team about his experience at the hotel and opened up the dialogue about a setting a similar standard in their restaurants. Instead of mandating the standard on day one, Cathy took a different approach. For over two years anytime someone would say thank you to him for any reason he would respond with, "It's my pleasure." People in the organization caught on and began to mimic his behavior. Before long, his example became everyone else's habit. Many years later, you can now walk in any Chick-fil-A and you would be shocked not to hear, "It's my pleasure." The standard was set by Truett, and it's carried out in the behaviors of every employee each day. It's wonderful to experience.

Cathy not only had a unique way of coming up with the standards at Chick-fil-A but also was creative in how he communicated them to get the correct behaviors of the employees. Another one of the defined standards at Chick-fil-A is that staff members are supposed to be friendly to customers and smile at them when they get to the front of the line to order.

Back in 1974, Cathy and the team were opening a new restaurant in Paramus, New Jersey. To mark the big occasion and to ensure it was successful, Cathy traveled to help open the store on its first day. Instead of just being a figurehead, Cathy handed out samples to potential customers who were unfamiliar with the now-famous chicken sandwiches.

On this particular launch day, Cathy noticed one of the team members working the register was not smiling at customers as they came up to place their order. He called over the store manager, "Jimmy, every time I look over I notice Jenny isn't smiling at customers when they place their order." Jimmy went right into "fix it" mode, and during a small break in traffic he pulled Jenny aside and told her to make sure she smiled when new customers came to place their order. But Jimmy's words didn't work. Cathy kept noticing Jenny wasn't smiling, so the next time he went back to refill his sample tray, he walked past Jenny and said, "How come every time I walk by, you are smiling?" The young employee looked at him and cracked a small smile. Cathy didn't stop there. Every time he got more samples, he would mention to Jenny, "Look at you always smiling." In a matter of 20 minutes, the two had a real connection. When he would look over at her, she would smile and almost laugh. Before long that smile on her face became permanent instead of just momentary.

It doesn't matter who it was or what had happened before: smiling at customers was and remains a standard at Chick-fil-A. Instead of lowering the standard because Jenny was unwilling to meet it or worse, firing her during her first day on the job, Cathy got creative and helped her meet the standard in a fun and unique way.

This is proof standards do not have to be complicated and no standard, regardless of how simple, should be assumed; it must be communicated. There is no denying how aligned Chick-fil-A's people are at creating a unique and differentiated experience for customers. At the core of this is their leaders and the standards they set for the team. Here is the best part: Chick-fil-A doesn't have a patent on it. You can and should leverage standards to align the behaviors of your team. When you do, I promise you will be on your way to getting the results you want out of others.

Route to Results

To understand exactly how leaders who build the best get consistently high results from their team, we studied and interviewed the leaders who scored the highest on LearnLoft's BTB Leader Assessment. A consistent pattern began to emerge.

The pattern was solidified even further for me when I was having dinner at a local restaurant. I said thank you to my waitress as she refilled my drink. "It's my pleasure!" she shot back. Never missing an opportunity to explore my curiosity, I responded, "Have you ever worked at Chick-fil-A?" "Yes, sir, I worked there for four years back when I was in high school. I haven't worked there in 10 years, but I never dropped the habit."

I knew, then, the pattern for consistently high results. High standards produce behaviors from people. Those behaviors, when practiced repeatedly, become a habit, and those habits lead to results (Figure 8.1). This pattern is what I've come to call the Route to Results.

FIGURE 8.1 The Route to Results

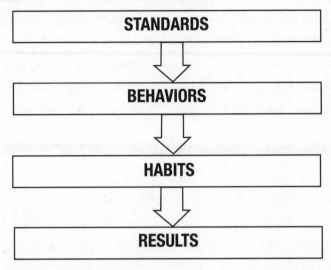

To continue the example of Chick-fil-A and to make the Route to Results come to life, the "It's my pleasure" standard for a new employee would look something like this. The standard is set on the first day: when a customer says "thank you," you reply with "My pleasure." Each time a customer does this, the new employee has to consciously decide to respond with "My pleasure." With some reminding by colleagues, along with positive reinforcement from the store operator when the new employee gets it right, it begins to feel like a comfortable response. After repeating the known behavior hundreds of times a day it will become a habit, and the employee will respond with "My pleasure" without even thinking. The habit creates a memorable experience for Chick-fil-A's customers, and as a result, they continue to visit Chick-fil-A, thus creating the desired business result.

Instead of focusing on results first, you must have the patience to follow the Route to Results. Start at the beginning by setting great standards, and the rest will follow.

The Route to Results, once understood and applied, will help you to align the behaviors of your team.

Breaking It Down

By definition, standards simply define what good looks like. The way I want you to think about them is slightly different. The leaders who build the best don't define what good looks like, they define what *great* looks like. When you define what great looks like for your team and communicate it correctly, these standards will produce behaviors and habits that are vital for achieving results.

First, a behavior is defined as the way in which one consciously acts or conducts oneself. The key word here is *consciously*. Each person walking the earth makes many decisions every day—the majority of them consciously. These can be impacted based on how we think or feel in a given moment.

Conversely, a habit is something done without thinking or subconsciously. Amber Selking, a performance coach, defined a habit so simply on the *Follow My Lead* podcast: "Something you do so often it becomes the very essence of your being."

A great example of a habit you can probably relate to is leaving your cell phone plugged in next to your bed. When you wake up, you reach for the phone and begin checking it without a second thought. It's something you do without thinking. It's a habit.

Traditionally habits are formed over time. Most people who agree with this believe it takes between 30 and 60 days for a behavior to becomes a habit. Turns out time isn't the only factor or even the most important factor. How *often* you repeat a behavior is what turns it into a habit. If a family moves from one house to another and the house they moved from had a traditional fence but the new house has an electric fence, would it take their dog 30 to 60 days to make staying inside the electric fence a habit? No, the behavior of going outside and not going beyond the electric fence would take just a couple of days (assuming the dog goes out four or five times a day). The same is true for people. While the more complicated behaviors might take more repetition than a simple behavior to become a habit, there is no doubt the habits in our lives lead to results.

Setting Standards

Have you ever driven over the speed limit? I suspect you answered yes because we all have. But have you ever willingly sped past a police officer? I'm guessing your answer is no. Why is this? Each state sets speed limits on roads to "define what good looks like." These are meant to keep not only you safe but others on the road as well. It is the duty of a police officer to enforce the standard by giving out tickets to those who do not adhere to it. The threat of punishment aligns the behaviors of drivers from all background with all different types of cars.

Now imagine for a minute your state decided to remove speed limit signs altogether. Drivers could drive as fast as they wanted on any given road. Would you still drive 25 mph in a school zone, or would you go 35 mph and just keep an eye out for children? My guess is you would pick the latter. The principle here is this:

> The instant you lower the standard is the instant performance begins to erode.

A great example of this that's easy to relate to is one that rental car companies made famous. If you have ever rented a car you know the standard is to return the car with a full tank of gas. If you decide not to meet the standard, they charge an astronomical amount to refill the tank. Sometimes it costs four times more than if you were to fill it up yourself. This standard and known consequence produces consistent behaviors from many different kinds of people. If the rental car companies were to lower the standard to return the car with the tank half-full versus completely full, renters would fill it up halfway instead of all the way.

Turns out all standards aren't the same. They come in three forms: policies, procedures, and merits.

- **Policy standards** typically come in the form of an organizational policy that rarely changes over time. These encompass safety rules or sexual harassment regulations that are rarely controlled by team leaders—these are hard lines. A great example would be this: on a construction site everyone, regardless of their role, must wear a hard hat. It is a standard that must be met. Policy standards may also be created and regulated by a power outside of your organization such as an association or board.

- **Procedure standards** are process-oriented things that could change over time. Think of it as a documented best practice, which can be followed exactly or modified slightly depending on the situation. A few examples are a complex business-to-business sales process, scripts for a Customer Service department, or how a team meeting is run. If you think back to Chick-fil-A, saying "My pleasure" after a customer says "thank you" is simply a procedure standard.
- **Merit standards** often are the most customized per leader. These tend to be value-oriented based on what the leader believes to be right or wrong—things like the golden rule, avoiding negativity, not allowing gossip, or going the extra mile for your clients.

Of the three forms of standards, you have the most control over procedure and merit standards. Focusing on these two will help align the behaviors and elevate the performance of the team. It's important to remember there is a fine line that you toe when setting standards. They are not meant to create power or elevate you above anyone else.

Creating Standards

In Building the Best workshops, I use a specific structure for the creation of standards. It goes as follows: Write down two standards that fall into the categories of policy, procedure, and merit. Keep it to a sentence or less to ensure a clear standard. Here are some examples:

Policy
- "Dress code: Dress appropriately for the day."
- "Misconduct: Legal or moral misconduct will never be tolerated."

Procedure
- "Inbound leads: Followed up on within the first business day."
- "Tactical weekly team meetings: Communicate what you've done, what you're working on, and where you need help."

Merit
- "Choices: Do what's right, always."
- "Positive attitude: You control your feelings about someone or something."

These are all short and powerful examples of standards that help produce behavior that is aligned across the team. In an effort to help you further, I want to go deeper into a procedure standard most employees hate: team meetings.

Mike Shildt took over as manager of the St. Louis Cardinals during the midpoint of the 2018 season. The team was playing well below expectations. Knowing the difficulty of his new job, Shildt introduced a new daily meeting that he called "ball talk." The purpose of "ball talk" was to huddle up as a team before games and brainstorm the following three things:

1. What went well the previous day's game?
2. What was needed to improve?
3. What can the team do to be successful in the game today?

The "ball talk" meetings usually last 10 minutes, but they have been known to go from 2 minutes all the way to an hour. Even though Shildt is in the room and prepared with notes from the previous day's game, it's the players who drive the discussion. One of his all-star players, Matt Carpenter, described it this way in an interview with ESPN: "It's like group therapy and really productive. It's something of value. I don't like just sitting in meetings, but we are getting things accomplished and getting better, I am all for it."

After the implementation of "ball talk" the Cardinals got much better. They ended with one of the best records in the league after Shildt took over as the manager, going 41–28 and narrowly missing the playoffs by a mere three games. Carpenter believed Shildt and "ball talk" were at the center of their transformation. "Mike has a way of bringing everyone together into the conversation. He shows he cares about people by writing hand-written notes, texts, and phone calls. He doesn't get emotional, panicked, he understands how hard the game is and doesn't live and die by the results. He took over a tough situation and really unified the clubhouse. He got guys to buy into what he wants."

There are many lessons to learn from a leader like Mike Shildt, but his implementation of the "ball talk" standard is a great one. This struck a personal chord with me because the first year leading my own team I really struggled to run productive meetings. For example, every Monday morning the entire team met and reviewed what we had going on that particular week. I spent the vast majority of the meeting talking. Each week the meeting would pass, and each week a little more energy was drained from the team. It was the hiring of Corey, our first remote team member, that caused a radical shift in our weekly meeting and the creation of a new standard. At the end of one particular meeting, Corey called afterward and said, "John, I appreciate you getting the entire team together every week, but I have noticed as an outsider that people aren't all that engaged, and you spend the majority of the meeting talking. In my previous role, we had a team meeting structure that people loved, not because it was shorter, but because it helped us all do our job better. Would you be open to me sharing it with you?"

Without hesitation, I said, "Please do." He went on, "Each meeting every member of the team comes prepared to discuss three things: what I did last week, what I am doing this week, and where I need help. We would go around the room quickly and everyone on the team was prepared, and most importantly my boss was able to help each one of us perform better each week by aligning with where we needed help." Instantly the lightbulb went off for me.

The next week, I introduced the new meeting structure to the team, and in less than three meetings we were in a groove. The meeting time went from two hours down to one, and people came prepared each week to play a major part in the meeting instead of sitting on the sidelines as bystanders. Over time, I have adapted the weekly tactical team meeting to follow this structure:

- **Step 1:** Small talk
- **Step 2:** Update progress toward team goal and meaningful wins from the prior week
- **Step 3:** Review team priorities on whiteboard
- **Step 4:** Each team member reviews their "done, working on, need help"
- **Step 5:** Motivational topic or vulnerability moment from John to team
- **Step 6:** Exit and execute

Like anything, the more familiar you become with something, the more ingrained it becomes in your behavior. Try using the meeting structure with your team as a standard and you will see a difference in behavior in just a few weeks.

If you already have a tactical meeting structure you like and you want to create other procedural standards, there are three questions you can ask yourself:

1. What's the desired end result you want from your team? (Outcome)
2. What's stopping the team from getting there? (Problem)
3. What can be done instead? (Standard)

The LearnLoft tactical weekly meeting standard is depicted in Table 8.1 using the three questions.

TABLE 8.1 Weekly Meeting Standard

	QUESTION	ANSWER
OUTCOME	1. What's the desired end result for the team?	Have more productive weekly meetings where people are engaged
PROBLEM	2. What's stopping the team from getting there?	John is doing all the talking and no one knows what to expect each week
STANDARD	3. What can be done instead?	Everyone comes to the meeting prepared to answer three questions: 1. What's the most important thing you accomplished last week? 2. What are you going to do this week to move the needle? 3. Do you need help?

Ideally, you will have as few standards as possible to get the desired behavior from your team. If you have to define every minute detail, then there is a good chance you have the wrong people on the team.

Communicating Standards

Setting standards is great, but if you don't clearly communicate them to your team you might as well not have come up with them in the first place. The late Pat Summitt definitely didn't make this mistake. The Hall of Fame Women's basketball coach had enormous success on the court over her 38-year coaching career at the University of Tennessee. Not only did she retire with 1,098 career wins and eight National Championships, but 25 of her former players and assistant coaches have gone on to major roles in coaching and basketball management. This success didn't happen by accident. It came in large part because Summitt was a master at communicating the standards of her program.

She had 12 standards for her teams at Tennessee, and she communicated them all the time. They were written in their locker room and made available for the team to see and read almost everywhere they went. Here are the 12:

1. Respect Yourself and Others
2. Take Full Responsibility
3. Develop and Demonstrate Loyalty
4. Learn to Be a Great Communicator
5. Discipline Yourself so No One Else Has To
6. Make Hard Work Your Passion
7. Don't Just Work Hard, Work Smart
8. Put the Team Before Yourself
9. Make Winning an Attitude
10. Be a Competitor
11. Change Is a Must
12. Handle Success Like You Handle Failure

She communicated these 12 standards in one-on-one meetings when they weren't being met as well as in front of the entire team to ensure they weren't forgotten. Ideally, you will communicate your own standards when taking on a new position or as new professionals join the team. While that is the ideal time, it's more likely you need to communicate your standards to a team you already lead in an effort to reestablish clarity and focus.

The old-school way of leadership would have this as a clear-cut exercise where you gather the entire team, announce the new standards, and send people on their way. The new model of communicating standards is much different. It is centered on knowing "why" the standards exist in the first place. The old saying, "Because I said so" isn't good enough in today's environment. For each standard you set for your team, it's critical you are able to articulate why it exists by tying it to one of two thoughts our brains are always evaluating: "gain" or "pain."

While there isn't a perfect answer to which one works better, the more effective you are at clearly articulating the "gain" or "pain," the better the adoption of standards will be. As an example, the Allstate insurance company uses both in TV commercials to drive the same outcome. In some commercials they highlight the Safe Driving Bonus Check if you are a client of theirs and you avoid accidents over the course of two years. The "gain" is that by aligning your behaviors to safe driving you will get a check from Allstate for your great behavior. Just a few minutes later, on a different channel, you might see a different commercial from the same company featuring "Allstate Mayhem": a fictional character who torments people or distracts them in order to create havoc so major accidents happen. This commercial creates a sense of fear or "pain" in the mind of the prospective customer.

Whether you have seen the Allstate commercials or not, the simplest way to think about "gain" is by answering the following question around each standard you have established.

What good thing happens to each person individually or the team as a whole if they live out the standard?

The simplest way to determine the "pain" is by asking yourself a slightly different question.

What bad thing happens to them or the team if they fail to live out the standard?

While this seems simple, you would be amazed at how many leaders fail to think about why the standard exists. Regardless whether you lean toward connecting why a standard exists to "gain" or "pain," the key is knowing the answer and being prepared to share it.

Putting It Together

Once you're ready to have the conversation with your team, either one-on-one or in a group setting, there is a simple four-step conversation framework you can use to improve the likelihood you are successful. It goes like this:

- Step 1: I realize I have failed you from a leadership perspective (Vulnerability)
- Step 2: Here's how I propose we solve it (Standard)
- Step 3: If you live out this standard, here is what will happen (Pain avoidance or Gain)

- Step 4: Do I have your commitment moving forward? (Buy-in)

This four-step approach adds two very important elements to the standards you have set and the pains or gains you have previously identified. First, it begins by creating a moment of vulnerability in front of your team. Too often leaders forget this very important piece and start the conversation with everything their team is doing wrong. When this happens the conversation almost automatically puts other people in a defensive position. Instead, by using a vulnerability statement like, "I realize I have failed you from a leadership perspective," you create a safe space by putting the blame solely on yourself. Secondly, you ask for their commitment to gain their buy-in to the standard moving forward. Instead of pushing or forcing some new standard on them, you are asking for their verbal commitment, which drastically improves the odds it will be lived out in their behavior.

Here is how it would sound if a new standard for your team was "Greet every customer with a smile."

"I have been doing some self-reflection about how I am leading, and I realized there was an area I failed you from a leadership perspective around the proper way to greet customers when they come into the store. To remedy the situation, I propose that anytime a customer comes in the store they are met with a smile from whoever is behind the counter, myself included. If we live out smiling at every customer, it's scientifically proven to enhance their shopping experience and will play a major factor in whether they come back soon. Since we have an aggressive growth goal this year and we all have a bonus if we hit it, it's imperative to create a unique customer experience, and it starts with a smile. Do I have your commitment moving forward that anytime customers come in they will be met with a smile, regardless of how you feel that particular moment?"

Getting Standard-Worthy Behaviors Consistently

Leaders who Build the Best brilliantly focus their team standards on setting the bar high. They constantly reward, recognize, and talk about these standards on an ongoing basis to ensure they get the right behaviors day in and day out.

In the next chapter I am going to cover holding team members accountable to standards; I'll say now that there is a simple and easy way to ensure people are living up to the standards set for your team.

Growing up, my family loved board games. It didn't matter the game, we played it with an intensity unmatched by any other family. We particularly loved Taboo, which Milton Bradley called, "the game of unspeakable fun."

Taboo is simple. The objective of the game is for players to have their team guess the word on the player's card without using the word itself or five additional "taboo" or forbidden words listed on the card. If the team member who is calling out the clues says one of the "taboo" words, a member of the other team smashes a red buzzer to make everyone aware of the infraction, which carries a one-point penalty. It is a fantastic game to play with friends and family. But I share this story about the game not because I love it but because of the act of hitting the red buzzer.

In the red buzzer lies a simple and mentally effective way to allow everyone on the team to call out others for behaviors that aren't standard-worthy and aligned to the group. I have seen some leaders keep the red buzzer from the Taboo game in a common place to remind everyone on the team of the standard, while others have a buzzer at everyone's workstation. The point isn't so much the physical act of buzzing someone. It is more to create a mental image and communicate the idea that behaviors that aren't in alignment with the standards do not go unnoticed.

The power of leveraging standards as a leader can transcend your time leading your current team. The people you lead will, without question, adopt many of the standards you set and carry them forward to lead in their future roles or even in their families. Team members come to respect the standards and uphold them on your behalf. But standards without accountability are just words, as we will see in the next chapter.

CHAPTER SUMMARY

- Principle 6: The instant you lower your standards is the instant performance erodes.
- Follow the Route to Results to align the behaviors of your team: Standards produce behavior, behaviors become habits, and habits lead to results.
- Standards define what great looks like.
- The instant you lower the standard is the instant performance begins to erode.
- Standards come in three forms: policy standards, procedure standards, and merit standards.
- You set the standards for your team.
- Explain why the standards exist by identifying the "pain" or gain."
- Reward, recognize, and talk about the standards on an ongoing basis to ensure you get the right behavior.

9

HAVE DIRECT DIALOGUES

"Leaders of consequence are clear about the shadow they cast because they want to create followership."

—JUD LINVILLE

Principle 7: Accountability Is an Advantage, Make It Your Obligation

There is no doubt now about the importance of setting and communicating standards. The challenge for many leaders comes when the standards aren't met.

In 1792 BC, Sin-Muballit gave up his throne of Babylonia to his son, Hammurabi, because of his failing health and a struggling people. The well-educated prince faced many areas of struggle and concern as his reign as king began. As a religious man he believed it to be his responsibility to bring righteousness to his land, destroy evildoers, and ensure that the strong people should not harm the weak. To help he compiled 282 laws to assist him in his ruling of the people and region. It was evident that Hammurabi understood that if people honored an agreement, they should be held accountable for falling outside of it. For example, Law 232 stated that if a Babylonian builder built a house using subpar materials and, for that reason, the house collapsed causing the death of the owner, the builder would be put to death. Harsh consequences, yes, but Babylonian buildings saw an immediate improvement in quality.

Law 232 is just one example of how the now famous "Hammurabi's Code" helped bring stability to the region and created a fairer system of checks and balances to how people treated each other. While there are issues with any set of laws and the interpretation of them, you would think a king who comes in and creates stricter punishment for breaking laws would be viewed as a bad ruler or, worse, face a rebellion. Quite the opposite is true. Not only did Hammurabi receive the honor of being declared a god within his own lifetime, but he was honored above all other kings of the second millennium BC. He was fondly remembered for bringing victory in war, bringing peace to the region, and most importantly bringing justice to those who had never had it thanks to what's now known as Hammurabi's Code.

While we could argue that many of the laws and consequences Hammurabi used are inappropriate today, there is no denying being a leader of consequence isn't a bad or negative thing when it comes to performance. In fact, it's required in order to build the best.

In many ways, the hardest element of leadership is being a leader of consequence and holding people accountable. Accountability is one of these words that has been used to the point that its meaning has been largely lost. The actual definition of *accountability* from BusinessDictionary.com is, "the obligation of an individual or organization to account for its activities, accept responsibility for them, and to disclose the results in a transparent manner." The word that has always jumped out to me here is *obligation*.

It is the obligation of all leaders to hold themselves accountable and help others do the same. Most people think of accountability in a negative way and believe because they are willing to fire someone that they are good at it. The truth is, accountability isn't only focusing on the negative; firing someone is one of the weakest forms of it. To go a step further, accountability can be used to praise and recognize team members who meet and exceed the standards set by a leader.

To ensure your success when holding others accountable, a plan of action is imperative. Trying to do so haphazardly will result in a downright disaster. The Acts of Accountability Model provides perspective.

FIGURE 9.1 Execution of Standards Continuum

FAILS   MEETS   EXCEEDS

The horizontal line in Figure 9.1 represents how a team member is executing a set standard on a continuum. People can fail, meet, or exceed a standard at any given time. You provide accountability by sharing disapproval when someone fails to meet the standards, acknowledging them when standards are met, and/or giving praise when standards are exceeded in the Acts of Accountability Model (Figure 9.2). Since each situation will be different, you then choose the intensity of accountability appropriate to the actions or behavior of a team member.

FIGURE 9.2 Acts of Accountability Model

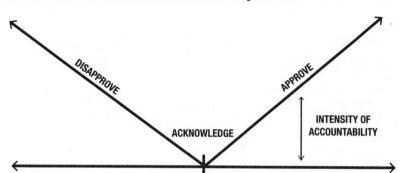

As an example, I have a standard that all team members "remain coachable." This means it does not matter how experienced you are or how long you have been at LearnLoft, it's everyone's responsibility to remain a student and listen to others in order to improve. If someone fails to meet the standard, I have a Direct Dialogue and share disapproval. Through the delivery of an open and honest conversation, we work together to determine what might be causing the shortfall and how the behavior can be modified going forward. If employees are coachable during a conversation, I acknowledge their coachability to ensure they maintain the mindset in future conversations. If they ask questions and take notes about how to improve, I give praise and recognition for exceeding the standard.

The Acts of Accountability Model provides an easy-to-understand framework for you to lean on to determine the appropriate accountability in a multitude of situations. Once you are able to quickly identify the behaviors from someone on your team, here is how you engage in disapproval, acknowledgment, and praise by using Direct Dialogues.

Direct Dialogues

I use the term *Direct Dialogue* because it's essential to be direct when pointing out how behavior can be improved or maintained and dialogue is an exchange of ideas, facts, and opinions of multiple people.

Direct Dialogues during moments of difficulty or even celebration can be uncomfortable, but consider the impact of not engaging in dialogue. If you withhold feedback in fear of a reaction, you are suppressing employees' potential by not sharing something that could help them on their journey, ultimately stunting their professional development. If you refrain from giving praise in fear of being perceived as corny or "soft," you are missing an opportunity to celebrate great work, which often leads to more of it in the future.

A meaningful Direct Dialogue requires the use of a three-part formula that has helped me and countless other leaders have successful dialogues with their people.

Standards + Evidence + Courage
= Direct Dialogue

If you have all three parts—standards, evidence, and courage—the interactions with your team members who fail, meet, or exceed the standard will happen naturally because you will be evaluating the standards set for your team, constantly observing evidence, and showing the courage to bring important things to their attention. Conversely, if one of them is weak or doesn't exist, your Direct Dialogue falls apart or doesn't happen altogether.

Since we covered setting standards in great detail in the previous chapter, I am going to assume you have them in place. The second element of the formula is evidence. There is nothing that will derail a Direct Dialogue with your people more than the lack of evidence. Because of this, you need to be prepared with facts and not feelings to support your disapproval, acknowledgment, or praise.

The evidence should be specific, detailed, and tangible. Each role in an organization is different, but here are a few of my favorite examples:

SALESPERSON

Standard: Each person controls what he or she can control, not the outcome.

Fails: Missed key research statistic for a big opportunity that was available on the web. Lack of preparation for initial sales conversation with inbound lead, no dedicated time spent working on the fundamentals of selling outside of active opportunities.

Meets: Added the new opportunity into the CRM on time, completed follow-up letter to the prospect with the correct information.

Exceeds: Interviewed three additional stakeholders in an account to gain insight that helped win an opportunity, added all documentation and the data from others into the opportunity in the CRM prior to the scheduled date.

BARISTA

Standard: Create a positive experience for customers and coworkers.

Fails: Greeted customers without a smile on Wednesday morning, came in 15 minutes late for a shift on Friday morning and left coworkers to run understaffed, missed two opportunities to help team members during the morning rush on Monday.

Meets: Made all drinks correctly and on time on Monday, cleaned bathrooms on schedule, greeted customers with a smile during all shifts, supported the team during peak hours by refilling low items from the storeroom.

Exceeds: Took time outside of work to get educated on coffee beans and shared the knowledge with customers this weekend, helped customers download the app on Monday so they could earn rewards for their purchases, told new team member she was doing a great job on Monday during a morning rush.

I realize these are specific examples that might be unrelated to your leadership role, but they all provide tangible evidence.

Many leaders claim they are "too busy" to spot this evidence. Just walking around the office or being attentive during a meeting isn't enough. Why? Because people are really good at straightening up or putting on an act when the boss comes around. Dedicate time on your calendar to proactively look for evidence each person is meeting, exceeding, or failing to meet standards. As you observe, take time to write down the specifics. The purpose isn't to seek bad behavior or find ways to micromanage. It is to capture evidence to encourage, reinforce, or improve the performance.

Once you have gathered the evidence of why a team member is failing, meeting, or exceeding standards, then you need the most significant element of the formula, courage. Courage is simply the ability to do something that frightens you. C.S. Lewis famously said, "Courage is not simply one of the virtues but the form of every virtue at the testing point, which means at the point of highest reality." Lewis got it right because each and every virtue a leader needs to possess will meet its testing point at some time.

Most leaders aren't comfortable with the idea of inviting a team member into a dialogue to share disapproval or praise, which is why courage is so necessary. If you fall into this category, ask yourself one simple question: "Will taking action help this person or encourage this person to continue something he or she is doing well?" If the answer is yes, it's time to move to the execution of Direct Dialogues to share disapproval, acknowledgment, or praise.

Sharing Disapproval

Many of the leaders whose style is to elevate have an innate talent for delivering successful dialogues with team members who fail to meet the standards. They instinctively position the conversation to lower the emotional tension, position evidence in a way that shows they care, and ask the right questions to promote self-discovery. Most of us who struggle with this particular skill need an aid, one that helps us emulate what the best do instinctually. The 6-Step Disapproval Dialogue helps you do this.

It's a straightforward set of steps that can be used to have more productive disapproval dialogues with your people in a short amount of time. The six steps include:

1. Set the stage.
2. Share evidence.
3. Allow response.
4. Talk impact.
5. Coach for growth.
6. Close with Actions.

Let's jump into the steps in detail, so you not only understand the steps but can apply them.

STEP 1: SET THE STAGE

The majority of disapproval dialogues fail because both parties involved believe they are on different teams instead of the same one. It's your job as a leader to set the stage for this dialogue so your team members know you are here to help not to hurt them. Start by stating a shared purpose statement to communicate you are on the same team, and you care about their development. It could sound like this: "We are here because we share the same goal. We both care about your personal growth and the development of our team." By opening with a strong statement showing a common purpose for improvement, the guard of your team member will go down, and he or she will be open to the rest of the dialogue.

STEP 2: SHARE EVIDENCE

We have all heard the saying "Results speak for themselves." But do they really? Take Mark McGwire, for example. He hit 70 home runs during the 1998 Major League Baseball season. At the time, this was the all-time record for a season. If you were Mark's baseball manager and only looked at results for evidence that season, you would have nothing except praise. But years later it came out that McGwire used performance-enhancing drugs, which improved his odds of hitting so many home runs during the season. Based on results, McGwire set a record. Based on the underlying situation, however, he didn't. This proves that results-based evidence is the wrong formula for long-term success.

In order to gain all of the needed evidence, observe both the current results as well as habits and behaviors on an ongoing basis. There are two things to look for within these behaviors and habits: will and skill.

Will = Attitude and positive motivation

Skill = Technical ability to execute the job

Will issues need to be addressed head-on, while skill issues need to be coached and developed. I will share more about coaching for skill issues later on in the book.

This is where the evidence you have collected about the areas of improvement comes into play because you will be listing off a few of the things that need to get better. Without facts, you will be stuck in a series of feelings that are ripe to be disregarded or, worse, countered with an alternative opinion. It could sound something like this: "I noticed Monday when your colleague Mike gave you ideas for improving your speed to complete the project, you immediately interrupted him and became defensive. This behavior of being uncoachable manifested itself again yesterday on our joint call with our client when you completely disregarded the feedback the client gave you about your work. Being coachable is a standard all of us are responsible for, including me. Is there anything going on I should know about because this isn't like you?" By laying out the evidence of multiple events in which the will-oriented behaviors failed to meet the standard, you provide clarity. This clarity will elicit some form of a response or rebuttal.

STEP 3: ALLOW RESPONSE
Some people tend to be better at receiving feedback than others. Their response will include an agreement, a defensive statement, silence, or an argument. Allow them to voice their response and listen intently as they do. Remain calm and stick to the facts and/or proof about your observations. As John Quincy Adams said, "Facts

are stubborn things." The exchange might sound something like this:

> TEAM MEMBER: "It was the client's fault; they
>   weren't clear about what they wanted."

> YOU: "I was on the first call with the client, and
>   they were clear about what they wanted.
>   You weren't coachable, and I am telling you
>   this because I have seen you be coachable
>   before. So, I was disappointed to see this
>   when I know what you are capable of."

By reiterating the facts and providing a statement of encouragement, you again offer a way to calm the emotions in the room and renew your shared purpose of growth and improvement.

STEP 4: TALK IMPACT

Since our brains are always thinking about either a pain or a gain, now is the time to get specific about the impact of team members' behavior on themselves or the team if this behavior continues. It could sound something like this: "When you aren't open to feedback or better ways of doing something, it slows us down and hurts our teamwork. We are only as strong as our weakest link." In a swift comment, you make your team member aware of how the behavior not only affects the member but the team as a whole. If you have specific stats or examples of what the behavior cost the team, this is the time to share it.

STEP 5: COACH FOR GROWTH

As you will learn in the next chapter, every person could be in a different stage of role development, but it's never a bad idea to ask a few great questions about how people plan to make changes. You can home in on open-ended questions that are focused on improving future outcomes. It could sound something like this: "What other approaches might you take next time?" or "What do you think we should do moving forward to ensure this doesn't happen again?" Both of these questions allow your team member to internalize and determine the best way to solve the problem moving forward. If the person doesn't have answers, be prepared to make a few suggestions or tell a story about how you weren't coachable at one point and what you did to overcome it.

STEP 6: CLOSE WITH ACTIONS

Now it's time to gain a mutual confirmation on what behaviors will change and how the team member plans on changing them. Talk in detail about the actions you expect in the future and if necessary the consequences if the behavior doesn't change. It could sound something like this: "Can we agree that you have room for improvement when it comes to our standard of remaining coachable? As a next step, I am going to follow up on your current projects on May 15th at 11 a.m. to see how you are doing with your colleagues and our clients. I will send you a meeting invite." By setting up a specific time and date to follow up, you show you are serious about inspecting what you expect. Once you have confirmed

158

the next step, now the real work starts. These are things like documenting the conversation in an e-mail, following up and following through on your commitments to inspect, and observing and reassessing improvement over time. Create a system that works for your schedule to allow this type of detail. Below are a few best practices:

- Send an e-mail summarizing the conversation with a meeting request for a future date included.
- Schedule a one-on-one meeting with a colleague who works closely with the team member to gauge behavior change.
- Provide educational content to the team member around behavior change.

In every workshop I deliver, the question always comes up, "This is great, but what about the consequence of losing their job?" While the threat of firing can undoubtedly be a consequence, I prefer to see outcomes that aren't so extreme. If you do choose extreme consequences (which I admit might be required at times), just know you have to have the courage to follow through if the behavior change isn't met.

Having a disapproval dialogue when someone isn't meeting the standard can be challenging. Often conflict will arise, or excuses will start flying from the person you are delivering the criticism to. Remember you are holding team members accountable to help them improve, so these dialogues must happen. Be direct, confident, and rely on the 6-Step Disapproval Dialogue to help you with both preparation and execution. Each situation and leader is different; the key is you are having the dialogue to help promote better choices to your team. You can go to buildingthebestbook.com/tools to download a copy of the 6-Step Disapproval Dialogue to help you.

Alternative Methods for a Disapproval Dialogue

Now that you have a clear pathway to have disapproval dialogues, you probably realize there isn't a one-size-fits-all approach. Not every leader does things exactly the same, but different methods can get similar results. There are two other methods I want to highlight.

A study done by researchers from Stanford, Columbia, and Yale explored the secrets of giving great feedback. They had middle-school teachers assign an essay-writing assignment to their students, after which students were given different types of teacher feedback.

To their surprise, researchers discovered that there was one particular type of teacher feedback that improved student effort and performance so much that they deemed it "magical." Students who received this feedback chose to revise their paper far more often than students who did not and improved their performance significantly. What was the Magical Feedback? This one phrase:

> "I am giving you these comments because I have
> high standards and I know that you can reach them."

This simple phrase provides the opportunity for you as a leader to reiterate your high standards while sharing your belief in others out loud. I have successfully adopted this phrase in all areas of leadership. I use it with my children, my coworkers, and even my spouse because it works.

Joe Maddon, a successful Major League Baseball manager and current skipper for the Chicago Cubs, has a unique way of handling these disapproval dialogues with his team members. When one of his players violates a team rule or isn't meeting the standards set by the coaching staff, he asks the player to get a nice bottle of wine and then open it with him in a one-on-one meeting. Thus he's dedicated time to the player to have the disapproval dialogue, while at the same time creating a deep sense of connection between the two of them. This unorthodox approach turns the act of sharing disapproval into an act of deep connection. It doesn't mean he isn't delivering the message to the player, but he understands the walls that can go up when delivering a message that someone might not like to hear. The environment can be just as important as the message itself. The key here is to find what works best for you and your team. Once you find out the message that works best, be consistent in delivering it because it is paramount to help improve the performance of individual team members and the group as a whole.

Becoming a leader who embraces the challenge of having productive disapproval dialogues isn't easy. But if you want to build the best, this is precisely the attitude and effort required. As I mentioned earlier, all accountability isn't negative. There is a form that comes off as neutral.

Acknowledging When Standards Are Met

Many of the below-average leaders I interviewed for the book responded to the idea of acknowledging when standards are met with the following: "Why would I do that? That is what they are paid to do." While I can understand where they are coming from, I found that leaders whose style is to elevate have the opposite mentality. When behaviors are up to the predetermined standards, these leaders take the time to acknowledge this fact. They continue to rely on the formula of Standards + Evidence + Courage = Direct Dialogue to ensure they share acknowledgment. Below are some of the most commonly used phrases these leaders use to show you how they do it:

- "Thank you!"
- "Well done!"
- "Good job!"
- "Looks good!"
- "I appreciate the work!"
- "Keep it up!"

Although this seems simple, choosing to use these words with your team can be a powerful tool. A large number of employees feel undervalued, underappreciated, and frustrated at work. Simple acts of acknowledgment go a long way toward helping employees feel the opposite of these negative emotions. It is important to note, you do not want to go overboard in praise and recognition or people will start to believe just meeting the standard is as good as they can do.

Giving Praise When Standards Are Exceeded

As important as sharing disapproval and acknowledgment are to creating a culture of accountability, it is equally important to give authentic praise and recognition when people go above and beyond the standard. Why? Because people have three basic needs—they need to feel well-liked, important, and appreciated. It is human nature. One way to help them fill these basic needs is to give them authentic praise. People of all generations, whether they admit it or not, like to be praised. Receiving recognition releases dopamine in the brain, making people feel good. Beyond that, dopamine has also been proven to create innovative thinking and promotes problem solving at work.

It is just like when you share a picture on social media that gets 100 likes or when someone leaves a positive comment on something you've shared. Those small recognitions make you feel good and make you want to keep doing it again.

Those leaders whose style is to elevate understand this. They continue to use the formula of Standards + Evidence + Courage = Direct Dialogue as their foundation for giving praise. In one of my coaching conversations with a client named Josh, he told me a story about someone on his team named Sharon. Due to some unforeseen circumstances out of anyone's control, Sharon noticed the company's website was offline at 6 p.m. While Sharon was not directly responsible for keeping the website up and running, she knew the standard Josh had previously set for his team, "It's never not your job."

Instead of shrugging it off as a problem she was not capable of solving and leaving it for the experts in the morning, she stayed at the office and worked relentlessly for over six hours navigating challenge after challenge to finally get the site online and live up to the standard. That same night, the e-commerce site sold multiple products—something it wouldn't have been able to do if the site was not online. The next morning, Josh had the courage to give Sharon praise and recognition in front of the group by saying, "Last night's effort made an immediate impact on our business, and I cannot thank you enough for your willingness to work hard and solve the problem."

Josh did as good of a job at giving authentic praise as Sharon did being proactive in her work. He relied on the standards set, saw the evidence of Sharon's effort, and had the courage to give praise. If that wasn't enough he also provided a window into exactly how to give praise by being definitive about when the behaviors occurred, sharing the impact it had on the team, and delivering it in front of the entire team. By doing this, he got everyone thinking about additional ways to exceed the standard in order to make the same kind of impact as Sharon on an ongoing basis.

Since giving praise isn't a strong suit for most leaders, I've developed the 3x3 Praise Model (Figure 9.3) to help. The first three parts of the model share what to do when giving praise. You can download a copy of the model at buildingthebestbook.com/tools.

FIGURE 9.3 3x3 Praise Model

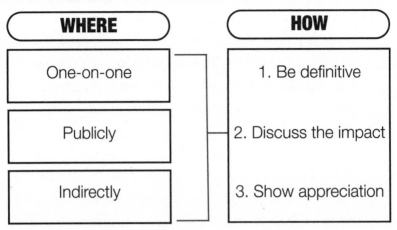

The model shows how and where to give praise. First, *how* to give praise:

1. **Be definitive.** Clarify what the team member did to exceed the standard. Instead of just focusing on the end result of the person's work, focus on the behavior that produced it.
2. **Discuss the impact of the behavior.** Highlight the impact the behavior had on the team, organization, or person. This is critical and often forgotten or assumed. Spell out what good things happened because of the person's extra effort.
3. **Show appreciation.** Tell the person how much it meant to you and how much you appreciate what he or she did for the team.

Now that you know what to do when giving praise, the other half of the 3x3 Praise Model focuses on *where* to do it.

1. **One-on-one.** Giving authentic praise directly one-on-one in person works best. While you can certainly rely on text messages, e-mails, or a Slack message, the most powerful way to give praise is face-to-face. If it is not possible to do in person, leverage these other communication methods to share praise.

2. **Publicly.** Giving praise one-on-one is great, but providing it in front of peers proves a platform to exude that praise beyond one individual and allows others to join in as well. It is almost like a built-in microphone. Not only does the person who deserves the praise get it from more people, but it promotes others on the team to emulate and mimic the behaviors that are receiving the praise.

3. **Indirectly.** It is easy to think about giving praise when the team member is present, but what about doing it when the team member isn't around? There is power in bragging about a team member's behaviors and performance to others as well. Most of the time it gets back to the individual you're praising, and now team members know you go out of your way to elevate them in front of others.

Most likely you already give praise to your people, so leverage the 3x3 Praise Model to think about additional ways of both where and when to give it to have the maximum impact. Giving praise costs you nothing, but it can mean the world to the person on the receiving end.

Taking Accountability to the Next Level

Taking the time to use the Acts of Accountability Model on a daily basis will improve your ability to identify the appropriate response and what level to impart. While I can't overstate the importance of this, the best leaders know accountability doesn't stop there. They are after something even deeper: a culture of accountability. Scott Frost knows a thing or two about this second level of accountability. He was hired as the head football coach at the University of Central Florida in 2015 with the team coming off of a 0-12 season under their previous head coach. Just two season later Frost guided UCF to an undefeated season, going 12-0 and being named coach of the year. Not only did he complete one of the great turnarounds in sports history, but he did it by focusing on his team. That success provided him the opportunity to return to Nebraska University to be the head football coach at his alma mater in 2018. When interviewed just a couple of months after starting his new job, Frost gave some insight to any leader trying to take accountability to the next level. "We need to train our leaders better. Once the team is holding each other accountable and the coaches do not have to do it, you've got a powerful team."

While I have zero doubt Frost will be able to do this at Nebraska, what he's striving to put into practice in order to create a true culture of accountability is something I call the Accountability Circle (Figure 9.4).

FIGURE 9.4 Accountability Circle

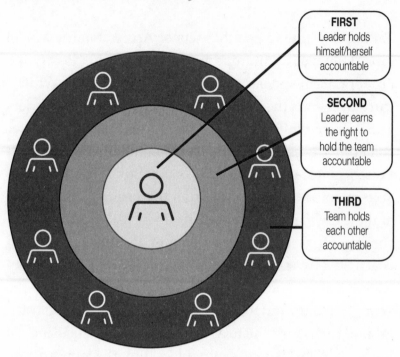

FIRST
Leader holds
himself/herself
accountable

SECOND
Leader earns
the right to
hold the team
accountable

THIRD
Team holds
each other
accountable

The first step is holding yourself accountable to meet
and exceed the standards you set to be a part of the
team. Then leveraging the great relationships you have
built with your people, you earn the right to hold others
accountable. It is intentionally built in a circle because
in order to take accountability to the next level the team
members themselves have to hold each other accountable
to the standards so the leader isn't always the one sharing disapproval, acknowledging when standards are met,
or providing praise when they are exceeded. You always
know you are getting near having a true culture of
accountability when you see teammates hold each other

accountable out of love and trying to help someone get better.

Now I do not pretend this is easy, but it is something every leader of a team or even a family should strive for. In order to begin this process, teach the Acts of Accountability Model and the Accountability Circle to your people.

Being a leader of consequence, where accountability is at the center of everything you do, will lead to improved performance. What you will also find is that not only will you be respected for it, but your people will appreciate and even end up demanding it.

CHAPTER SUMMARY

- Principle 7: Accountability is an advantage, make it your obligation.
- Being a leader of consequence isn't a bad or negative thing when it comes to performance.
- It is the obligation of all leaders to be accountable to themselves and help others do the same.
- The Acts of Accountability Model provides an easy-to-understand framework for you to lean on to determine the appropriate response in a multitude of situations.
- Clear Standards + Evidence + Courage = Direct Dialogue

- The 6-Step Disapproval Dialogue includes set the stage, share evidence, allow response and rebuttal, talk impact, coach for growth, and move to actions and consequences.
- Will issues need to be addressed head-on with direct feedback, while skill issues need to be coached and developed.
- The 19 words of Magical Feedback: "I am giving you these comments because I have high standards and I know that you can reach them."
- Simple acts of acknowledgment go a long way toward helping employees feel valued and appreciated.
- People have three basic needs: they need to feel well-liked, important, and appreciated.
- Giving praise costs you nothing, but it can mean the world to the person on the receiving end.
- Being a leader of consequence, where accountability is at the center of everything you do, will lead to improved performance.

10

DEVELOP
THE PEOPLE

*"Coaching is unlocking people's
potential and helping them learn
rather than teaching them"*
—JOHN WHITMORE

Principle 8: Coaching Unlocks Potential and Elevates Performance

For his eighth birthday, a boy named Bradley received his first basketball hoop. This gift solidified and nurtured his love of the game. As a freshman in high school, Bradley woke up early each day to practice. His hard work paid off, landing him a spot on the varsity team. Bradley shattered many school records and was eventually named an all-conference player in the state of Indiana. Despite his success in high school, no big-time college programs took notice. Bradley took his talents to a small university named DePauw. Quickly, Bradley earned the role of team captain in his senior year as he proved his worth not only as a player but a leader.

After graduating college, Bradley left the game he loved behind. Securing an entry-level corporate job, it began to sink in how much he missed being on the court. Bradley knew in his heart that he had to chase his dream of coaching basketball. Despite the opportunity for upward career mobility, Bradley said goodbye to the business world, taking a volunteer coaching position at Butler University.

Shortly after joining the program, Butler's then-assistant coach Todd Lickliter threw young Bradley into the fire by having him pull together game tapes and analyze them for the other coaches and players. It didn't take long for Lickliter to realize the potential in Bradley because of his work ethic, determination, and ability to complete his work at a high level. So Lickliter continued to add additional responsibilities after he hired him to a full-time position. Bradley eventually worked his way up the ranks and earned the title of head coach at Butler. His first season saw such success that Bradley was signed to a seven-year coaching contract.

In 2013, after six years as head coach and multiple trips to the Final Four, Bradley departed Butler University for an opportunity in the NBA. The Boston Celtics signed him as head coach. Bradley had made it. Bradley, best known as Brad Stevens, is the second youngest NBA head coach in basketball history. Stevens has successfully led the Celtics to the playoffs every year since his second season with the franchise.

Albeit it is clear that Stevens himself is a talented leader, it is those he was surrounded by while chasing his dreams that make his story so poignant. During a speech to captains of local high school teams, he expounded upon this, saying, "The people I like being around the most, are the ones who are invested in me and strived to help me get where I wanted to go. It's selfish but it makes me feel better and you know whether you fail or succeed, it has a purpose. That's exactly what I try to do for my assistant coaches and players because it was so important for my life and career."

• • •

Leaders who truly elevate others have never been more important than they are today. While a team can function autonomously, a strong, dedicated leader plays an integral role in pushing people to new heights of development. They do this by focusing on coaching their people for role development and going beyond the role.

Coaching for Role Development

Swimmer Michael Phelps learned early that you cannot reach your full potential without the help of others. The most decorated Olympian of all time won 28 medals, 23 of which are gold. During his preparation for the 2008 Olympics. Phelps put in 365 days straight of practice and then proceeded to win an Olympic record eight gold medals during the games.

While most people are aware of his achievements, most don't know his coach Bob Bowman was by his side for every single one of those 365 training sessions. Phelps noted later, "Without Bob Bowman, I would have had no shot at achieving the records I've achieved or winning the medals that I've won."

I know it's unlikely you coach Olympic athletes for a living, but the takeaway still applies. Focusing your coaching efforts on the progression of each team member's development in their current role helps them to reach their full potential. Depending on your current leadership role, you could have an entire team in the same exact role or you could have team members in various roles. Regardless of which situation applies to you, part of your job in the development of your people is to help them progress in whatever role they are currently in.

While there have been numerous models and research done around the development of a particular skill, I've found it much more valuable for leaders to evaluate each person's development in their current role. To help you do this, I will outline four clear stages a person moves through in a position or role (Figure 10.1 and Table 10.1). Well-tuned leaders are able to identify where team members are currently in their development and align their coaching appropriately. This allows for a platform through which each team member can flourish and grow. The goal is steadfast: Help your people reach a stage of development that exceeds where they are today.

FIGURE 10.1 Four Stages of Role Development

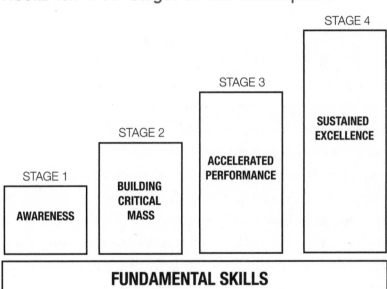

Stage 1: Awareness

Individuals are made aware, either by another person or through self-discovery, of the important fundamental skills they need to develop in their current role. They then do a mental assessment of their current proficiency level in each of the fundamental skill areas. Once this is established they evaluate the ways and/or resources available to help them make progress. The time spent in this stage can be anywhere from one day to six months.

Individuals in the Awareness stage often experience feelings associated with fear of the unknown. While taking on a new role can certainly be exciting, if a clear road map of skill development for the role isn't determined in short order, it can quickly become overwhelming.

Stage 2: Building Critical Mass

Individuals begin building critical mass in their role as they acquire knowledge and get the opportunity to advance their skills within the position. They advance quickest in this stage when they get both the opportunity to watch others apply the skills effectively and the opportunity to practice the skills while being watched by someone else. Eventually, confidence is built and individuals will start to apply the concepts learned by themselves. Their proficiency in all the skills involved in the role will often double time after time in this stage. Time spent in this stage ranges from three months to two years.

It's common for individuals at this stage to struggle to acquire the skills as learning takes place. This causes them to doubt themselves and their ability to perform in the role. Often the harder a role is, the more likely a person will want to give up. Those who get past this hurdle begin gaining the knowledge and confidence required to progress.

Stage 3: Accelerated Performance

The role becomes easier for individuals to execute and they are able to fully execute the job responsibilities on their own at a high level. Because of this, their confidence continues to increase and the ability to add on or modify skills contributes to the streamlining of related daily tasks. Errors are much less frequent during this time. Often individuals are able to teach less-experienced teammates how to do the job by transferring the knowledge and experience they have gained. As great as this is, many people stop developing their skills at this stage. There's a tendency for people at this stage to believe they've learned all they can and settle into false a sense of security. Time spent in this stage can last anywhere from 12 months to 10 years.

It's common for individuals at this stage to have strong feelings of accomplishment and satisfaction in their development.

Stage 4: Sustained Excellence

The role is mastered. There is no lack of knowledge, as individuals at this stage have a well-rounded understanding and ability to execute at the highest level. This doesn't mean they always perform all of the tasks required to do the job without error, but they sustain excellence by having the ability to self-correct when they make mistakes. Their sustained excellence can earn the individual the title of "industry expert." It often can take 5 or 10 years to enter this stage, and sometimes it's never achieved regardless of time.

It's common for individuals at this stage to experience boredom, loss of focus, or even disinterest because the climb to sustained excellence seems over. Many individuals make the mistake of not continuing to expand their role beyond their daily job requirements.

TABLE 10.1 Feelings Associated with the Four Stages of Role Development

	STAGE 1 **Awareness**	STAGE 2 **Building Critical Mass**	STAGE 3 **Accelerated Performance**	STAGE 4 **Sustained Excellence**
Description	Discovering and understanding the skills required to be successful in the role	Acquisition of knowledge begins and ample practice is required to develop necessary skills	Job performance improves significantly and errors rarely happen	The role is mastered and expertise is displayed on a daily basis
Feelings	Fear of the unknown and being overwhelmed	Doubt in themselves and their abilities.	Strong emotion of accomplishment and satisfaction.	Boredom, lack of interest, and complacency
Time	1 Day–6 Months	3 Months–2 Years	1–10 Years	5–10 Years

The Fundamental Skills

At the foundation of each of the four stages, there is a need for a relentless focus on the fundamental skills required to progress in the role. Alan Stein Jr., author of *Raise Your Game*, knows this firsthand. He shared a story with me during an interview about a time he was a counselor at

NBA legend Kobe Bryant's basketball camp in the prime of his career. Stein was hungry for knowledge, so he approached Kobe at the end of practice to ask if he could watch his workout the next day. Kobe agreed and told him to be there at 4. Somewhat confused, Alan responded and said, "Kobe, we have practice with the kids tomorrow at 4." Without hesitation, Kobe said, "4 a.m."

Not wanting to be late, Stein arrived at the gym the next morning by 3:30 a.m. As he walked in the gym the lights were already on, the ball was bouncing, and Kobe was in a full sweat 30 minutes prior to his scheduled workout with his trainer. Throughout the workout, Kobe was meticulous about his movements and repeated them over and over again from slow motion to full speed. At the end of the practice, Stein thanked Bryant for the opportunity. He could not help but inquire about something, though. "Kobe," he said, "if you don't mind me asking, I'm a little confused. You're the best player in the world and the entire session you and your coach worked on what most players would consider fundamentals in a very deliberate manner." Bryant looked at Stein and without hesitation responded, "How do you think I got to be the best player in the world?" What many would consider "insignificant" Bryant saw as incomparable.

Now I know you are most likely not one of the best basketball players in the world. Let's say you lead a sales team. You should know the fundamental skills salespeople must deliberately practice in order to perform at their peak level: things like taking control of an initial conversation, asking great questions, discovering customer pain, building a vision, or establishing rapport. Your sales team should then be using deliberate practice outside of selling time to work on and sharpen their skills in these areas in order to move through the Four Stages of Role Development. You should then be aligning your coaching to where each individual is in the four stages to help them develop.

Deliberate Practice

I previously mentioned deliberate practice multiple times on purpose. Malcolm Gladwell, in his book *Outliers*, quotes psychology professor Anders Ericsson as saying that scientific studies show 10,000 hours are required to achieve the level of mastery associated with being a world-class expert—in anything. Unfortunately, Ericsson says Gladwell misinterpreted his research and that 10,000 hours of merely repeating the same activity over and over again is not sufficient to catapult someone to the top of their field.

Ericsson's finding from over three decades of research, which he highlights in his book *Peak*, says that deliberate practice is the key to achieving high levels of performance. This is extremely important because contrary to common belief, your own biggest strides toward sustained excellence in the skills required to be an effective leader will not be correlated with simply the amount of time leading. Instead, you must know the fundamental skills required to be an effective leader and then practice them in a deliberate way in order to get better faster. No one can do this for you because the development of skills is a lot like physical fitness: it simply can't be outsourced. Each person is ultimately responsible for the development of his or her own skills.

The same is true with any job, and the skills associated with performing at a high level.

Aligning Your Coaching to the Four Stages of Role Development

Michael Phelps' coach, Bob Bowman, said in a now-famous quote, "When I first started coaching, I only had a hammer so everything looked like a nail. That is incredibly effective, but it will wear you out. You cannot be other people's motivation. Now I understand, I still have a hammer, but I also have logic, I have a pat on the back, and I have empathy. So you want to add to your toolbox because it takes different tools to reach different people."

Just like Bowman, you need a different set of tools and methods to coach individuals depending on where they are in the Four Stages of Role Development—Awareness, Building Critical Mass, Accelerated Performance, and Sustained Excellence.

Here are some ideas for how to align to where people are and coach them at each of the Four Stages of Role Development (Figure 10.2, Table 10.2):

FIGURE 10.2 Coaching to the Four Stages of
Role Development

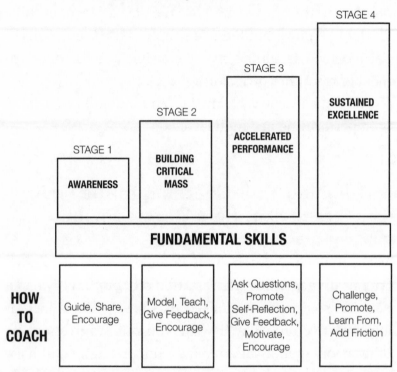

Coaching for Awareness

Team members who are in the Awareness stage require your help in discovering the skills they need to develop to even get started. It is best if you have clearly identified the specific skills required to perform the job so there are clear expectations. If left up to chance, there is a high likelihood a person without much experience will focus on the wrong things. As an example, a good golf coach working with a beginner is going to explain in the first lesson the importance of focusing on the most foundational elements of a golf swing like grip, posture, and alignment.

In our Building the Best workshops, participants create a Role Development Plan to ensure new team members are able to increase their awareness immediately. You can download an example at buildingthebestbook.com/tools.

Coaching While Building Critical Mass

Team members who find themselves building critical mass require hands-on development and interaction. It is your duty to teach and model the skills required; then be patient and provide encouragement. Create a safe environment for team members to get the opportunity to execute on their own even if that means they fail. This is a necessary part of the process because people who do not engage in failure struggle to learn and grow. This means you will have to challenge the voices inside their heads that are providing doubt and fear. Coach them up through encouraging words and moments of affirmation.

If you do not have the knowledge to teach or model a specific skill required to do the job, it is not game over. It's vital that you are educated enough to know which direction you should guide this individual in to further the person's development in this particular skill.

My own experience with this was one that presented a great learning opportunity. A member of my team was pursuing the skill of coding to be able to manage our website. I had no experience in coding and wasn't a resource of knowledge to teach or model it. Instead, I ensured open time on his calendar and encouraged him to take online courses to develop his proficiency at the skill during working hours.

We live in a world that's constantly evolving, and as people grow or roles morph and expand, people need to acquire new skills. If you foster a development mindset in your team members, they will be open to adding new skills to their toolbelt.

Coaching During Accelerated Performance

Delivering the answer to a question outright is quick and effective. However, it does nothing to encourage an individual's development at the Accelerated Performance stage. You must reject your natural instinct to solve every problem and instead leverage questions to pull the answers out of your team members. During an interview Michael Bungay Stanier, the author of *The Coaching Habit*, explained this very well. He told me, "Managers should stay curious a little bit longer and rush to advice giving a little bit slower." By taking this approach you are forcing team members out of their comfort zone and encouraging them to be more self-reflective.

Having productive coaching conversations with an individual can easily lead to the implementation of this practice. Using open-ended questions while focusing on useful outcomes free of judgment are the most effective.

Here are some examples:

- What can I do to help you?
- Can you tell me about that error?
- What do you think we should do to create the best result for everyone?
- Walk me through your thought process.
- What other approaches might you take next time?

Coaching in Sustained Excellence

In her book, *Build an A-Team*, author and speaker Whitney Johnson noted, "At the end of the day, boredom and laziness get disrupted by people who are more motivated and eager to surpass the competition."

While achieving sustained excellence in a job and the skills associated with it is exciting, this is the hardest stage for a leader to coach. Individuals at this level are likely to begin taking their hard-earned skills for granted. Keep an eye out for new challenges, job promotions, or opportunities for them to teach others. Adding friction such as new tasks or having them solve a difficult problem will keep them interested. Most importantly, if they begin to lose excitement, remind them of the purpose behind their work and the reason the execution of their job matters so much to the team and beyond.

Challenging those who have sustained excellence can come in many forms. Here are a few examples:

- Have them teach less-experienced team members who are learning the skill.

- Encourage them to share their expertise in a public way: writing for industry magazines, starting a blog or podcast, or even educating others in the organization.
- Allow them to seek public speaking opportunities.
- Add new job responsibilities.

TABLE 10.2 Coaching to the Four Stages of Role Development

	STAGE 1 **Awareness**	STAGE 2 **Building Critical Mass**	STAGE 3 **Accelerated Performance**	STAGE 4 **Sustained Excellence**
Description	Discovering and understanding the skills required to be successful in the role	Acquisition of knowledge begins and ample practice is required to develop necessary skills	Job performance improves significantly and errors rarely happen	The role is mastered and expertise is displayed on a daily basis
Feelings	Fear of the unknown and being overwhelmed	Doubt in themselves and their abilities.	Strong emotion of accomplishment and satisfaction.	Boredom, lack of interest, and complacency
Time	1 Day–6 Months	3 Months–2 Years	1–10 Years	5–10 Years
Coaching	Guide, Share, Encourage	Model, Teach, Give Feedback, Encourage	Ask Questions, Promote Self-Reflection, Give Feedback, Motivate, Encourage	Challenge, Promote, Learn From, Add Friction

Everything we have covered around coaching up until this point has to do with ensuring that people are performing at the highest potential in their current job function or position. Before we move on to coaching beyond the role, I want you to think back to the story of Brad Stevens and his professional journey. If the first basketball coach he ever worked with had kept him in his current role or didn't believe in his potential, Stevens might not have pursued more. The next "Brad Stevens" could be on your team—are you missing an opportunity to develop him or her?

Going Beyond the Role

As he looked down, the flashlight on his head illuminated his wristwatch, 5:20 a.m. He thought, "Is anyone going to come today? Will I do this on my own?" Sore from yesterday's run, he stretched his legs long in front of him. One car, then a second and third pulled up. Looking again to his watch, he saw that only minutes had passed. There were soon 15 men standing in front of him clad in shorts and T-shirts ready to work out. He knew the scene well, having worked out with these men, in the same manner, dozens of times, but today he was blanketed by uncertainty.

With sweaty palms and a cracking voice, he addressed the group.

"Good Morning. I am Cadillac, a former football player, so it's time to get your mind in the game. We are going to start with 50 high-knees, followed by 20 mountain climbers, 20 diamonds, 20 slow squats, 10 burpees, Jacob's Ladder hill runs, Oklahoma wheelbarrow pushes, 40-yard dashes, and we will end with three 100-yard runs."

It surprised him how fresh in his mind this routine was. Then again, he had been rehearsing his delivery in his mind for weeks. Just prior to beginning, Cadillac made one final announcement, "I have been working out with you for less than a month and this is my first time leading you. I am honored. Let's go get it." Inspired, the excited group of men let out a big, "huuhaa" and followed suit.

Cadillac wanted these men to push themselves beyond their own borders. He kept them focused and demonstrated the moves to those who were struggling. Offering words of encouragement, he challenged them to dig deeper and find that place of inner determination. As the final round subsided, the cohort of tired men formed the "Circle of Trust." Cadillac thanked each of them for their participation. Just before parting ways, the entire group rose to their feet and gathered in a tight group. Putting their hands on the shoulders of the men next to them, Cadillac closed with a short prayer.

As the group broke, Dredd, who had invited Cadillac to be a part of the group a month earlier, approached him. Giving him a big sweaty hug, Dredd said, "You did an excellent job and I am proud of you. You made F3 proud today by influencing men to movement. You clearly remembered our motto 'We don't leave anyone behind, but we also aren't going to leave you where we found you.' Have a blessed day."

What began as a Saturday morning activity between a small group of like-minded men has become an incredible example of individual development. Dave Redding, or Dredd, and Tim Whitmire, known as OBT, made the decision to leave an overcrowded workout group in 2011 and start F3. Several years later, over 18,000 men in 26 states have joined forces to do the same each week. F3 is named for Fitness, Fellowship, and Faith. Drawn in by the aspect of "fitness," "fellowship" is the glue that keeps the participants coming back while "faith" encourages them to explore service. The mission of F3 is simple: "To plant, grow, and serve small workout groups for the invigoration of male community leadership."

It costs nothing to join, and every workout is free of charge, open to all men, held outside regardless of the elements, and peer-led. Because it's peer-led, each man who participates eventually leads his respective group through a workout. From the beginning, Redding and Whitmore knew this was critical because deep down inside every man has the desire to lead. Part of F3's job is to scrape away the vines and weeds to reveal to men the leader they really are. Thus, they help create more leaders instead of just followers.

F3 doesn't stop at helping people develop by leading workouts. It produces a weekly blog, *F3 Nation*, that is used to transfer knowledge around leadership to its members all across the country. The leadership principles members teach are woven into every event, race, or mud run they do together. On the surface, it's easy to say F3 has done incredible things to keep men fit and healthy at a critical age in a man's life, and that's definitely true. But when you look at the most important thing the group does, it's building, developing, and encouraging the best version of each man in all the biggest areas: life, faith, health, and family. While F3 is just for men, there is also a fast-growing group for women called FiA, which stands for Females in Action, that has the same passion for developing the best version of women in similar areas.

• • •

Groups like F3 and leaders like Dave Redding and Tim Whitmire are special because they exist to develop people beyond the job. Part of your role as a leader if you are going to build the best is to go to this level. One of the best ways to do this is by understanding your people on a deeper level.

Align to the Dreams and Goals of Your People

Think back to the example of Jason Lippert and his company LCI earlier in the book. When they began to make progress on their high turnover rate by moving it from 115 percent to 35 percent in a three-year period, they didn't settle. Instead, they continued searching for ways to get better. One of the leadership coaches introduced an idea from the book *Dream Manager* by Matthew Kelly. The idea was simple: the key to motivation for employees was not necessarily the promise of a bigger paycheck or a title, but rather the fulfillment of a personal dream.

This struck a chord with Lippert. He knew if he wanted to have a meaningful impact on his people, it would require knowing what they ultimately wanted to achieve beyond their immediate role. As it turned out, many of the employees at LCI did not have a dream on their radar. Working paycheck to paycheck, they were making between $12 and $18 per hour and did not have the time or money to proactively think about a personal goal or dream. Lippert and the team had other ideas. They hired people to a new position called personal development coaches. Their job was not only to help team members flesh out their personal dreams and goals but to act as an accountability partner in helping to make them a reality.

In less than two years, the personal coaching program is now a companywide initiative called Dream Achievers™. Its mission is to educate, equip, and empower LCI employees to live more intentional and engaged lives through personal coaching and connection, to help transform business and society. The program has hired additional personal development coaches to hold one-on-one and group coaching sessions that seek to build productive mindsets in team members as they work toward accomplishing their goals and dreams in life.

By the first quarter of 2019, the program had reached over 1,000 LCI team members, resulting in over 300 large-scale dreams being achieved and a 92 percent retention rate. Dreams achieved included things like weight loss, debt reduction, improved marriages, and enhanced emotional well-being.

Since you probably do not have a program similar to this in your organization or personal development coaches to help you uncover the dreams of your team, it's critical you grasp how important it is to understand and cultivate goals, dreams, and aspirations. While it may seem a little odd to coach your people beyond the role they are in, ask yourself this question: "How are you going to contribute to their long-term success and well-being if you don't know what each person ultimately wants to do, become, or achieve?" The truth is, you cannot. It's more likely you will end up using their hard work and effort in their current role to help you achieve *your* professional dreams instead of theirs.

Leaders who build the best coach their people beyond their role by doing these three things:

Uncover Goals, Dreams, and Aspirations

If asking your team about their dreams isn't something you've done before, you may find it difficult to broach the subject. And if people aren't expecting it, they may be scared to voice their true desires.

In situations like this, I always go back to legendary football coach Lou Holtz. The year was 1966, and Holtz was hired by Marvin Bass to come coach at the University of South Carolina. He and his wife spent every dollar they had on the down payment for a new home to quickly get settled in Columbia in preparation for the birth of their third child. A month after he started, Coach Bass resigned to take a job in professional football, leaving Coach Holtz unemployed. Holtz's wife had always been a great encourager of him, so to lift his spirits and get him back on track she bought him a copy of *The Magic of Thinking Big* by David Schwartz. The book explained clearly, "The reason people don't get up and go do things each day is because they don't have clear goals. And to be accurate in goal setting you have to take a piece of paper and a pencil and write down all the goals you wish to achieve."

As legend has it, Coach Holtz started writing down his goals and dreams; before long he had come up with 107 clear and defined goals. When his wife got home one evening, he shared his goals list with great anticipation and excitement. As she finished reading the list, she looked up and said, "Honey, this is great but I don't see 'get a job' on the list." So instead of 107, it became 108. To date, coach Holtz and his wife have completed 102 of the 108 goals on the list.

Now, I share this story not just because it made a big impression on me but because it's an awesome story to share with your team. Sharing a real story like this increases the odds team members will open themselves up to writing down their own goals, dreams, and aspirations. In our Building the Best workshops we have leaders complete an exercise in which they write down their goals or dreams within the context of five categories: body/soul, family, career, finances, and excitement.

It is important to note that this exercise isn't about checking the box. Instead, it must come from a place of authenticity and getting people to think and communicate specific things they want to do or achieve. You can download the exercise worksheet at buildingthebestbook .com/tools.

You can use something as specific as this or, if you are comfortable enough, you can simply schedule a one-on-one meeting with each person on the team and ask them questions such as these:

- Is there someone whom you admired or aspired to be like because of the work they did or the person they were outside of work?
- If you surpassed this person, how would that make you feel?
- What kind of things would be happening in your life if you did?
- Are there any challenges going on in your life outside of work you want to solve or improve?
- What is a trip you haven't been on that you would like to make happen?
- Is there a role or job inside of the business you aspire to reach or grow into?

Refine and Get Specific

Pilots do not track their flight course directly from point A to point B. They aim for something north of their destination in order to land where they intend. This is the perfect way to think about your role in refining and getting specific with your people's goals and dreams. You must ask people to aim higher and be specific about what they aspire to achieve. I have found that size is relative based on whom you are talking to when it comes to goals or dreams. But what isn't relative and is of utmost importance is getting specific about what those goals or dreams are.

The first round of writing down or verbalizing a person's goals tends to be rather vague. Typically I see things like, "Go on a diet," "Help others," or "Make more money." While these aren't bad aspirations, they are far from specific and clearly achievable. Part of your job in coaching people is to challenge them to make the goal or goals achievable. The only way to do this is to ensure that when the goal is written down, you can clearly answer whether it has been or could be achieved with a yes or no. The revised list would be, "Lose 20 pounds by December," "Coach a Special Olympics basketball team," "Make $100,000 next year."

Encourage and Help

Encouragement is rocket fuel for confidence, and confidence fuels perseverance during adverse times. Achieving any goal or dream requires changes in behavior and sticking with those changes when it gets hard to continue. Part of your responsibility is to be an encouraging voice in people's head by leveraging words like:

- "You will," "You can," and "You have the talent to . . ."
- "Don't quit, you are on the cusp of making it."
- "Now is your time. Don't stop."
- "You are going to do great things, keep it up."

While these might sound corny, they are important words to hear from another human being. But words by themselves won't get people where they want to go. They also might require your help and assistance depending on the dream. Remember, you didn't get to where you are today without the help of others, and you could be that person for the people you lead.

Coaching people beyond their role isn't easy, and it often doesn't show immediate results. Which means most people will ignore this part because they believe it's less important than other things they do. Instead of taking this mindset, embrace the challenge of understanding your team members' goals, dreams, and aspirations and relish the opportunity to help make them happen. Channel your inner F3 mentality and build the best.

CHAPTER SUMMARY

- Principle 8: Coaching unlocks potential and elevated performance.
- There are Four Stages of Role Development: Awareness, Building Critical Mass, Accelerated Performance, and Sustained Excellence.
- What's most important about the stages of role development is how you align with them in order to best coach your people.
- Don't miss out on the opportunity to help your people achieve their goals.
- Ask your people about their goals, dreams, and aspirations. It creates long-term results.
- You must ask people to aim higher and be specific about what they aspire to achieve.
- Encouragement is rocket fuel for confidence, and confidence fuels perseverance during adverse times.

PART IV

NEVER FORGET THESE

11

USE THE Cs

*"The art of communication is
the language of leadership."*

—JAMES HUMES

Matthew Kauth had always been a passionate and faith-filled man. When he chose to enter the seminary to become a Catholic priest, it didn't shock those who knew him best. It was during his seven years of education in various seminaries throughout the world when he discovered a leadership gap in the church. He described the gap as a "lack of patrimony." This is anything that is "handed down" in an institution—part of its tangible and intangible "wealth." He felt this two-thousand-year-old profession was lacking a structure to help its men develop into the priests God had called them to be.

All great leaders, when they find a problem, set out to fix it, regardless of how big it may seem. After years of work and research, Father Kauth determined he couldn't solve the problem on the macro level, but he could do something on the micro level. In a meeting with his bishop, Peter Jugis, an opportunity to create a brand-new seminary presented itself. Together they decided this institution, called St. Joseph College Seminary, would be built on patrimony—something radically different from its predecessors.

St. Joseph College Seminary wasn't immune to the common challenges new ventures face when it came to financing, location, and most importantly men to enroll. Father Kauth was taking an enormous leap of faith to start a seminary without knowing if anyone would show up. He then noticed a trend that young men were more likely to discern a call to the priesthood upon graduating high school instead of after college.

In 2016, during St. Joseph's first year, it had space for up to eight men, and exactly eight signed up. The next year, it created capacity for eight more men, and nine signed up. Since one had left the previous year, the seminary was at capacity again, this time with sixteen young men. The success didn't stop there. The third year, eight more signed up and the seminary was able to find space for that exact amount again. The success rate was surprising to Father Kauth, who knew how difficult it was for a young man between the ages of 18 and 25 years old to commit to exploring a religious calling. What started as a small dream in one man's head became a reality during one of the most turbulent times in the history of the Catholic Church.

The Way You Feel
Is the Way You Live

Every person experiences a roller coaster of emotions at one point or another during his or her life. Many make whimsical and capricious decisions based on their response to those emotions, and one bad decision can lead to a chain reaction of poor decision making. Because of this, the way you feel tends to be the way you live. Father Kauth didn't want to live like this, and he definitely didn't want the seminarians at St. Joseph's to live that way either. He wanted them to live toward a purpose, and this meant having to say no to a lot of things in order to achieve something greater.

Father Kauth was keenly aware that these young men were up against some difficult outside forces, but he knew that structure and consistency would help them avoid living by these swings of emotion. Consistency comes in many forms, but Father Kauth knew in order for St. Joseph's to be successful, his leadership and the routines of all those involved had to be close to unchanging. The seminarians had to have a routine they could count on, so they could feel secure and be a part of something. This meant setting up a daily structure that better resembled one of a Navy SEAL than a man studying for the priesthood.

- 5:30 a.m.: Bell rings
- 6:00 a.m.: Mental prayer
- 6:30 a.m.: Lauds
- 7:00 a.m.: Holy Mass
- 7:45 a.m.: Breakfast
- 8:15 a.m.: Classes
- 1:00 p.m.: Lunch
- 2:00 p.m.: Recreation
- 3:00 p.m.: Free time
- 4:00 p.m.: Latin
- 5:30 p.m.: Vespers and rosary
- 6:15 p.m.: Dinner
- 7:00 p.m.: Study
- 8:15 p.m.: Confession and grand silence
- 9:15 p.m.: Reading
- 10:15 p.m.: Lights out

As rigorous as this schedule is, it gets tougher. The group practices grand silence from 8:15 p.m. to 8:15 a.m., which includes handing in their cell phones and speaking to no one. Outside of a Sunday afternoon, they don't watch any TV or listen to music.

When the men arrive at St. Joseph's, they instantly hate the schedule. They find it overbearing and have difficulty conforming to the structure. But after a couple of weeks, the consistency yields contentment and achievement. Father Kauth believes people live on achievement and want to see themselves doing something worthwhile.

While the consistent daily schedule is important, the communication between the leaders of St. Joseph's and its seminarians can't go unnoticed. Father Kauth knew that everything leaders do is communication and each transmission of communication whether it be verbal or through body language has to be received in the best mode of the receiver. When I attended one of their private evening prayer sessions, I was blown away by how the group recited Latin songs and prayers in sync. There was a vibrancy and commitment that was contagious. The only way for the seminarians to be in this kind of unison was for it to be taught and communicated in the way they best received it. While there is no doubt there is a higher calling at play, there are two important lessons someone who is building the best can take from Father Kauth and St Joseph College Seminary. Each day leaders must focus on consistency and communication.

Consistency

Consistency is the steadfast adherence to principles, truths, or standards of behavior. It's often confused with intensity, but being consistent is far more important. Take for example brushing your teeth. What keeps your teeth healthy is not the intensity with which you brush them, but rather the act of doing it twice a day. The same is true in leadership. Steadfast adherence to principles and standards of behavior will make you a more successful leader and help you build the best possible version of your team. If you lack consistency, you create a sense of uncertainty and doubt in others that is almost impossible to overcome.

While this might seem obvious, being consistent with your principles or standards of behavior can be one of the hardest things for you to master. Just think about all the things you need to be consistent with day in and day out. Showing up to work on time; work ethic; being an example for your people to model; setting goals and achieving them; building strong relationships; setting and maintaining standards of behavior; coaching others; being relentless, diligent, thoughtful; the list goes on. All of a sudden, being consistent looks like a pretty tall order. Instead of allowing it to overwhelm you, keep one word in the forefront of your mind: steadfast. The more you are steadfast with your leadership approach each day, the better the overall outcomes will be.

Communication

In order to get people to want to follow you and join you on your journey, you must be able to speak to your audience. I am not breaking any news here, but it's impossible to be a highly effective leader without being a great communicator. As we examined leaders who truly elevate others from all industries, one of the main places of separation from all other styles of leadership was their ability to communicate at the highest level. They all had an ability to talk about their agenda in a way that spoke to their people's emotions and aspirations. They knew hearing or seeing what they had to share wasn't enough. Their message had to be personally meaningful to their people, or it wouldn't be carried out or comprehended.

A significant communication skills gap was identified in a recent study by LinkedIn of human resources recruiters and hiring managers. Of the respondents, 94 percent said a person with good experience and exceptional communication skills is more likely to be elevated to a position of leadership than someone with more experience but weaker communication skills.

Communication has more to do with the audience than the person doing the communicating.

In order to help you be a more effective communicator, I am going to focus in on something I call the 3 Cs of Successful Communication. Your words have to be Clear, Concise, and Conclusive. Regardless whether you are using oral or written words, each and every message should pass through the 3 Cs test.

Be Clear

When was the last time you finished reading an e-mail or listening to someone talk and at the end, you were completely confused by what they meant or were asking you?

Lack of clarity is all too common. While people are listening or reading they are scanning to figure out two things: should I care, and what am I supposed to do? While these sound like deep questions, you process them naturally without much thought at all. This is why the clearest communicators will almost always win in the long term because people know exactly what is being asked of them and what the communicator is trying to say.

To ensure your written communication in the form of e-mails, text messages, or Slack messages are clear for your intended audience, ask yourself these questions before hitting send:

- Is it clear what I am asking them to do after they finish reading it?
- Am I asking for more than one or two things?
- How simple or complicated is what I am asking?

Similarly, when speaking, consider if you're answering the same questions. Unlike written communication, most verbal communication happens in real time, which doesn't allow for a natural moment of pause to evaluate the clarity of your message. This means having clarity when speaking requires a lot of practice and repetition. A great way to evaluate how clear you are with others is to ask a simple question prior to moving on: "To make sure we are on the same page, can you let me know what you heard?"

Obviously, every situation doesn't allow for this question, but it's a great way to test the clarity of your messages following a one-on-one conversation.

Be Concise

If clarity is the most important thing when it comes to effective communication, being concise is a close second. People are obsessed with having everything right now, so the more concise you are the more likely you are to get your message across to others. If that wasn't enough, the human brain is wired to conserve energy and attention. If you aren't concise, your audience's brain will start to change its focus to conserve the energy and attention they have left for something better.

While concise certainly could mean shorter or more brief in nature, you can still have an hourlong meeting, a 20-minute video, a 500-word e-mail, or a 40,000-word book that is concise. Use as few words as possible to get your point across. If being concise isn't your strong suit, here are a few tricks to help you:

1. **Twitterize it.** Twitter became famous for only allowing 140 characters per tweet. The company has since expanded a tweet to include 280 characters, but the exercise remains the same. Give

yourself a character limit in written forms of communication and make yourself convey the message at hand in less than 280 characters. Carefully edit your messages down to include only what's critical.

2. **Turn on the timer.** Disrupt HR is an organization created to give a voice to human resource professionals and their ideas. Instead of copying the popular TED Talk format, the founders of Disrupt HR chose a completely different way for presenters to share their ideas. Each presenter is given five minutes, uses 45 slides, and those slides automatically change every 15 seconds. You can use the concept of turning on the timer as a way to ensure you are concise. At your next team meeting set your phone time for five minutes, and when it goes off you are finished talking. After just a few meetings like this, you will find yourself communicating at a level of consciousness you never thought possible.

Be Conclusive

Donald Miller wrote in his book *Building a StoryBrand* that our brains are constantly thinking about whether or not what they are reading or listening to is going to help them survive or thrive. In other words, if what you are communicating isn't connected to helping your audience survive or thrive, they aren't going to pay attention for long. While this can be tricky, leaders who build the best are intentional about using their words in a conclusive way that helps the recipient determine the potential positive or negative outcome of their response.

Today's modern professional is being constantly bombarded with everyone's best life on social media. Finding ways to connect with people's heart or mind about what good could happen if they do something or what bad thing might happen if they don't do something is crucial to keeping them engaged and choosing wisely. A few questions you can use to evaluate if your messages are conclusive include:

- Have I communicated why this is important to the person receiving it?
- Have I communicated potential benefits in the future?
- Have I communicated what bad things might happen if action isn't taken?

Leveraging the 3 Cs of Successful Communication will without question help you better connect with and be on the same page with your people. Get in the habit of asking yourself, "Am I being clear, concise, and conclusive?"

Hold On . . . It's Not Just Verbal or Written Communication

You are communicating all the time as a leader regardless if you think you are. Researcher Albert Mehrabian published a book, *Silent Messages,* in 1971 that coined what came to be known as the 7 percent rule. In the book, Mehrabian discussed his research on nonverbal communication used by salespeople. He concluded that prospective buyers based their assessment of credibility on factors other than the words a salesperson spoke—the prospects studied assigned 55 percent of their weight to the speaker's body language and another 38 percent to the tone and music of the person's voice. They assigned only 7 percent of their credibility assessment to the salesperson's actual words.

Over the next four decades, researchers and organizational psychologists have argued over the validity of Mehrabian's research in today's time. Regardless of what side of the fence you sit on, the important thing is to remember that your communication with others goes beyond just verbal or written communication. Be aware of and focus on expressing positive and encouraging body language as much as humanly possible.

Most every seminary, Catholic or not, has as much if not more resources than what Father Kauth started with. What has separated him as a leader and the seminary as a whole is a consistency and a communication style that is unmatched by other seminaries. Not only is it fueling the seminary's growth, but it's a model we all can learn from and leverage with our own teams each and every day.

CHAPTER SUMMARY

- The way you feel tends to be the way you live.
- Each and every day leaders must focus on consistency and communication.
- Consistency is steadfast adherence to principles, truths, or standards of behavior.
- Steadfast adherence to principles and standards of behavior will make you a more successful leader and help you elevate others.
- Communication has more to do with the audience than the person doing the communicating.
- Communication goes beyond written or verbal, it's also body language.
- There are 3 Cs of communication: clear, concise, and conclusive.

12

KEEP THE DOOR MOVING

*"The best time to plant a
tree was 20 years ago.
The second best time is now."*
—CHINESE PROVERB

magine you're an architect of a new commercial building. It is in a busy, up-and-coming part of town, and there are only two rules for the project: the entrance has to be able to keep horses out, and no one who enters or exits will have to open the door for someone else. What kind of entryway would you design?

Normal hinge doors will not work. Neither will a sliding one. Your only real option is a revolving door. As legend has it, the revolving door was created by Theophilus Van Kannel in 1888 in response to these exact specifications. While there are other great benefits to revolving doors, such as keeping out noises and controlling airflow, what is wonderful about this invention is that the revolving door does not care who pushes it. It does not automatically refuse to move because of someone's gender, race, or age. It does not have an expiration date, but rather keeps turning, day in and day out, when people go through it. The revolving door has two openings; one where you enter, and one where you exit.

Leadership is similar. You'll achieve nothing unless you take the initiative and responsibility. If your actions can inspire, empower, and serve in order to elevate others over an extended period of time, then you can lead wherever you are. You can lead at work, in your family, or in the community. It is my hope that the stories, ideas, strategies, and tools in this book will help you to keep your revolving door moving. Aspire to let people in, then come out on the other side better than they were before.

The PTS Method: "Prepare to Serve"

There is a simple yet highly effective method to help remind you to lead this way. It's what I call the PTS Method and is something I have put into practice in my own life, both at work and at home. It's really a way to flip your mindset away from "you" to elevating others. Here is how it works.

When you change environments, you say to yourself, "Prepare to serve," and then you put it into action. An example of changing environments would be when you get out of your car or off the train from your commute to work. Prior to walking into the office, you would simply say to yourself, "Prepare to serve." Without thinking much after that or trying to do anything drastically different, you will have your people's interest top of mind.

Try it when you walk into your house at night. Before walking through the door, say to yourself, "Prepare to serve." You will be amazed at how willing you are to help out your spouse or your kids simply because you have changed your thinking. When you put the PTS Method into practice every day, you'll quickly find yourself becoming a leader that your people want to emulate and follow.

If you have difficulty remembering, set a notification on your calendar to remind yourself of the PTS Method. Or try hanging PTS signs on doors as a visual reminder. The important thing is to find something that works for you and reminds you to "prepare to serve" when you change your environment.

I would be lying to you if I told you I was always able to remember the PTS Method. Leading other people is hard, and I make mistakes every day. I disappoint my team and I think about myself too much at times. I fail to serve, empower, and inspire others, and you will, too. This journey will never be a perfect one. There is no ultimate destination, but rather a constant state of improvement to reach. In moments of difficulty, I want you to reference the following:

Nunc Coepi

I am a faith-based man. Because of this, I like to weave reading and growing in my faith into my daily habits. I once came across a video of NFL quarterback Philip Rivers. He was being interviewed about the Latin phrase *Nunc coepi*, which he wears on his hats and shirts during interviews. The phrase means, "Now I begin."

I found myself watching this video over and over because of this phrase. It stuck with me profoundly and has since become a part of my being. Day after day, I think about applying this saying in my faith walk; in the kind of husband I want to be; in the kind of parent I want to be; and in the kind of leader I want to be at work. *Nunc coepi* has given me the freedom to lose any guilt about my prior mistakes, errors, or poor thinking. It has been a vehicle I've used to transport me on my leadership journey. It has allowed me to forgive more, write better, and be more intentional.

In many ways, I don't care how you have been leading up to this point. I want you to remember *Nunc coepi*,

"Now I begin," each day. It will help you start the day fresh and lead better in the present moment.

E + R = O

As someone who did not take my education seriously until I was in my midtwenties, I have become an avid reader and listener in order to play catch-up. Many books and podcasts have had a major impact on me, but one idea in a multitude completely changed my perspective. It started when I read Viktor Frankl's book *Man's Search for Meaning.* Frankl was an Austrian neurologist, psychiatrist, and Holocaust survivor. While being tortured in the Auschwitz concentration camp and watching people die both mentally and physically, he found that he still had the power to choose how to react to his circumstances. This gave him the power to survive. He wrote, "Between stimulus and response there is a space. In that space is our power to choose our response. In our response lies our growth and our freedom."

While Frankl's book and story made a profound impact on me, I found a formula that compounded his insights in Urban Meyer's book *Above the Line.* It followed Meyer's story of coaching the 2014 National Championship football team at Ohio State University. In the book, Meyer shared a formula he had learned from Tim Kight of Focus 3: E + R = O, which stands for Event + Response = Outcome. The formula contains the simple idea that there are many events that happen in our lives; it is how we respond to those events that ultimately determines the outcome.

The idea, while new to me at the time, has been around for centuries. Marcus Aurelius, the famous Roman emperor and Stoic philosopher, discovered a similar idea during his life, which ended in AD 180. He wrote in one of his letters, "Our actions may be impeded . . . but there can be no impeding our intentions or dispositions because we can change and adapt. The mind adapts to its own purposes the obstacle to our acting. The obstacle to action advances the action. What stands in the way will become the way."

What Aurelius meant, much like Frankl and Meyer, is that we control very little of what happens to us in our lives, but we do control how we respond to those events. It's a simple idea that can take a lifetime to master. Whether this is the first time you have learned of E + R = O or it's a reminder, the better you get at controlling your response the better your outcomes will be.

This idea provided such clarity for me in life. It has helped me have much better outcomes to the hundreds of events that happen in my life on a daily basis because I now understand I only control my response, not the events. Starting at the ripe age of three, I teach the concept to my kids to help them process, deal with, and produce better outcomes when outside events happen them. While it certainly is more difficult for a child to process and handle, it is never too early for someone to start taking control of how they respond to events. It's my hope you will pass this along to your team, kids, or spouse because life isn't fair. If there is one thing I know for sure, you and everyone in your life will have many events happen to you in your life that you have no control over. What you can control is how you respond.

Attitude and Effort

"There are two things you can control every day: your attitude and effort." When Jay Wright, head coach of the men's basketball team at Villanova, said this to me during an interview, it became like concrete in my mind. Be it because of the perceived credibility of his words to me or the fact that I had looked up to him for so long, they took hold. It immediately became evident to me that most of us do not take advantage of this fact that we can, in a world that is so often out of our hands, control these two things.

The word *attitude* simply means a settled way of thinking or feeling about something or someone, typically one that is reflected in a person's behavior. While this is important for anyone to know, it is especially important for you. As someone who leads other people, if you grasp and take control of your thoughts and actions about events that happen or your feelings about someone else you will have a major advantage. While this sounds easy in practice, it's extremely difficult to live out every day.

When there is a member of the team they just don't see eye to eye with, most managers will allow their attitude to turn negative about that person and either hold a grudge against the person or put the person on the bottom of their team totem pole. While conventional thinking would confirm this is okay, it's the opposite of what the best leaders do. They don't allow those initial feelings or judgments about a team member to become an ingrained way of thinking. Instead, they reject them and allow themselves to lean into that person.

Effort, on the other hand, is simply a vigorous or determined attempt. Effort is about being relentless in everything you to do. Too many leaders give up too early because the job is hard and refuse to put their maximum effort in every day. The reason this lesson has taken such a hold on me is because it's an excellent lesson to teach anyone in life. Every person on my own team controls their attitude and effort every day. It's not something I can do for them, instead, I can make sure I control my own in a positive way, teach them the principle, and then just repeat it often. To give you an idea of how much I repeat it, every day when I drop my six-year-old off at school, the last thing I ask him is, "What are the two things you get to control today?"

● ● ●

Leadership is hard. So hard, most people avoid it, and those who embrace it often fail. That doesn't mean you shouldn't pursue it or should give up, because failure is not final. Failure is a part of leadership, which means failure must become feedback, When you make mistakes, don't beat yourself up, learn from it. If leadership were easy, everyone would be doing it. I am encouraged that you have embraced the responsibility of leadership and have rejected passivity. This world needs you to lead in a way that elevates others. The fact that you got to this point in this book shows me you are serious about becoming a better version of yourself, and that's the hard part of the battle. But it is not the whole battle. Occasionally thinking about the principles in this book is where most people will stop, but not you. You are going to be different; you are going to turn knowledge into wisdom and make a positive impact in the lives of many people. When you do, I can't promise immediate results or instant positive reactions from your team, but I can promise you are doing the right thing. The impact you make on others will go beyond your wildest imagination. It will be a force on this earth well after you are no longer here because the people you lead will remember and eventually elevate those they lead.

Anytime you see revolving doors, I want you to ask yourself a simple question: "Am I leading correctly?" Remember, leadership is about serving, empowering, and inspiring in order to elevate others over an extended period of time. You are a perfect person to live this out every day.

CHAPTER SUMMARY

- Nothing is achieved unless an individual takes the initiative and responsibility.
- You can lead wherever you are.
- Remember the PTS Method = Prepare to Serve.
- Remember *Nunc coepi* each and every day; it will help you start the day fresh and lead better in the present moment.
- E + R = O, Event + Response = Outcome
- You control very little of what happens in your life, but you do control how you respond to those events.
- There are two things you can control every day: your attitude and effort.
- Leadership is hard—so hard, most people avoid it, and those who embrace it often fail. That doesn't mean you shouldn't pursue it or should give up. Failure isn't final, failure is feedback.
- Leadership is about serving, empowering, and inspiring in order to elevate others over an extended period of time. You are a perfect person to live this out every day.

References

I am a human and make mistakes. My wife would tell you I make many mistakes. Either way, I have included a detailed list of references and citations for each chapter of the book. While I have done my absolute best to give credit where credit is due, it's possible I missed a few things. If you find anything that I have misrepresented or have forgotten, please let me know by e-mail (info@ learnloft.com), and I will get it updated as soon as possible. In addition to the references on the pages to come, you can find a full list of updated references and corrections at buildingthebestbook.com/references.

INTRODUCTION

Jan-Emmanuel De Neve, Slava Mikhaylov, Christopher T. Dawes, Nicholas A. Christakis, and James H. Fowler, "Born to Lead? A Twin Design and Genetic Association Study of Leadership Role Occupancy," *The Leadership Quarterly*, 2013; 24 (1): 45.

The State of Leadership Development: The Time to Act Is Now, 2015, http://www.brandonhall.com/mm5/merchant.mvc.

Corporate Executive Board (CEB), *Why Managers Fail*, 2016, https://news.cebglobal.com/press-releases?item=67148.

CHAPTER 1

John Y. Simon, *The Union Forever: Lincoln, Grant and the Civil War*, 2012, http://www.abrahamlincolnsclassroom.org/abraham-lincolns -contemporaries/abraham-lincoln-and-ulysses-s-grant/.

The American Institute of Stress, 2011, https://www.stress.org/.

Shira Ovide, "MF Global: Likely Among the 10 Biggest Bankruptcies Ever," *Wall Street Journal*, 2011, https://blogs.wsj.com/deals/2011/10/31/mf-global-likely-among-the-10-biggest-bankruptcies-ever/?mod=e2tw.

Jeff Skilling. "Jeffrey Skilling," Wikipedia, 2019, https://en.wikipedia.org/wiki/Jeffrey_Skilling.

Bethany McLean and Peter Elkind, *The Smartest Guys in the Room: The Amazing Rise and Scandalous Fall of Enron*, 2003.

Jennifer Robison, "Turning Around Employee Turnover," Gallup Business Journal, 2008, https://news.gallup.com/businessjournal/106912/turning-around-your-turnover-problem.aspx.

CHAPTER 2

"Financial Crisis of 2007–08," Wikipedia, 2019, https://en.wikipedia.org/wiki/Financial_crisis_of_2007%E2%80%932008.

Casey Crawford. John Eades, "How to Build a Company You Truly Want to Work for with Casey Crawford," *Follow My Lead* podcast, LearnLoft Season 9: Episode 8, 2018, https://followmylead.libsyn.com/how-to-build-a-company-you-truly-want-to-work-for-with-casey-crawford.

Jason Lippert. John Eades, "The Best Leadership Example I Can Find with Jason Lippert," *Follow My Lead* podcast, LearnLoft Season 16: Episode 1, 2018, https://followmylead.libsyn.com/the-best-leadership-example-of-i-can-find-with-jason-lippert.

Bob Chapman. Truly Human Leadership: Bob Chapman at TEDx-ScottAFB, TED Talk 2017, https://www.youtube.com/watch?v=njn-lIEv1LU.

John Maxwell, *Laws of Leadership* (Thomas Nelson, 1998).

Peter Browning. John Eades, "Leadership Lessons from the Boardroom with Peter Browning," *Follow My Lead* podcast, LearnLoft Season 5: Episode 3, 2018, https://followmylead.libsyn.com/leadership-lessons-from-the-boardroom-with-peter-browning

CHAPTER 3

Chris Low, "Meet the Man Who Always Believed in Dabo Swinney," ESPN, 2017, http://www.espn.com/college-football/story/_/id/18441434/clemson-tigers-dabo-swinney-national-champion-thanks-man-hired-believed-him.

Blake & Mouton, Managerial Grid, 1964, https://en.wikipedia.org/wiki/Managerial_grid_model.

Carol S. Dweck, *Mindset: The New Psychology of Success* (New York: Random House Publishing Group, 2007).

CHAPTER 4

George MacDonald, *At the Back of the North Wind* (New York: Airmont Publishing Company Inc., 1966). "To be trusted is a greater compliment than being loved."

Robert Caslen. John Eades, "Leveraging Character in Your Leadership with General Robert Caslen," *Follow My Lead* podcast, June 2019, https://followmylead.libsyn.com/leveraging-character-in-your-leadership-with-general-robert-caslen

Henry Blodget, "LinkedIn's CEO Jeff Weiner Reveals the Importance of Body Language, Mistakes Made out of Fear, and One Time He Really Doubted Himself," *Business Insider*, September 22, 2014, https://www.businessinsider.com/linkedin-ceo-jeff-weiner-on-leadership-2014-9.

Character in Trust. This story was told to me by Maria Weist during an in-person interview on January 18, 2018.

Jim Estill. John Eades, "Success Habits of Effective Leaders with Jim Estill," *Follow My Lead* podcast, November 2017, https://followmylead.libsyn.com/the-success-habits-of-effective-leaders-with-jim-estill.

Cameron DaSilva, "Watch: Sean McVav Gives Passionate Speech About Leadership to Young QBs," *Rams Wire*, July 16, 2018, https://theramswire.usatoday.com/2018/07/16/nfl-los-angeles-rams-sean-mcvay-speech-passion-leadership-qb-collective/.

Guy Raz, "Live Episode! Starbucks: Howard Schultz," *How I Built This* podcast, NPR, September 28, 2017, https://one.npr.org/?sharedMediaId=551874532:554086519.

Lazlo Bock, *Work Rules! Insights from Inside Google That Will Transform How You Live and Lead* (Twelve, 2015).

General Caslen, character in leadership. Capt. Garrison E. Haning, "Caslen's Career Comes Down to Character," Association of the United States Army, September 14, 2018, https://www.ausa.org/articles/caslen%E2%80%99s-career-comes-down-character.

CHAPTER 5

Chip Brewer and Callaway Golf. John Eades, "Demonstratively Superior Pleasingly Different with Callaway Golf CEO Chip Brewer," *Follow My Lead* podcast, Season 9: Episode 1, 2018, https://followmylead.libsyn.com/demonstratively-superior-pleasingly-different-with-callaway-golf-ceo-chip-oliver.

Google's Project Aristotle. Julia Rozovsky, "The Five Keys to a Successful Google Team," re:Work, November 17, 2015. https://rework.withgoogle.com/blog/five-keys-to-a-successful-google-team/.

Andy Stanley, "Leaders who refuse to listen will eventually be surrounded by people with nothing helpful to say." 2016, https://www.goodreads.com/quotes/9021237-leaders-who-don-t-listen-will-eventually-be-surrounded-by-people.

Daniel Coyne, *Culture Code: The Secrets of Highly Successful Groups* (New York: Penguin Random House, 2018).

Social relationships linked to mental health, morbidity, and mortality. Julianne Holt-Lunstad, Timothy B. Smith, and J. Bradley Layton, "Social Relationships and Mortality Risk: A Meta-analytic Review," *Plos Medicine*, July 27, 2010, https://journals.plos.org/plosmedicine/article?id=10.1371/journal.pmed.1000316.

Positivity Project. John Eades, How to Lead Yourself First with Mike Erwin, *Follow My Lead* podcast, Season 13: Episode 2, 2018, https://followmylead.libsyn.com/how-to-lead-yourself-first-with-mike-erwin. To learn more about these programs, see: https://posproject.org/.

Heliotropic effect. Kim Cameron, "The Universality of the Heliotropic Effect," TED Talk 2018, https://www.youtube.com/watch?v=YLTyFMnVZgs.

"Row the Boat," P.J. Fleck. "Gopher Talk 101 with P.J. Fleck: 'Row the Boat,'" https://www.youtube.com/watch?v=ZoGqXuQK0Vc.

Todd Weiden, "Run this town." Todd Weiden started this mantra as a VP for SunTrust Bank. For more on Todd, see: https://vimeo.com/user43801266.

CHAPTER 6

"Don't be afraid to give up the good to go for the great." John D. Rockefeller, https://en.wikiquote.org/wiki/John_D._Rockefeller.

Joanne Tate and Trinity Episcopal School. John Eades, "Follow Your Joy with Joanne Tate," *Follow My Lead* podcast, Season 16: Episode 6, 2018, https://followmylead.libsyn.com/follow-your-joy-with-joanne-tate.

Chick-fil-A mission statement. "Who We Are," Chick-fil-A, https://www.chick-fil-a.com/About/Who-We-Are.

Chick-fil-A performance, April 2017. https://www.eater.com/2018/4/2/17187976/chick-fil-a-growth-expansion-sales.

James Franklin, "Core Values," https://twitter.com/coachjfranklin/status/635763399113228288.

Skookum core values. Joe Ryan of Skookum shared this with me during an in-person interview on January 15, 2019.

Amy Reid, "Myles Munroe: 'The Power of Vision,'" CBN, http://www1.cbn.com/books/myles-munroe%3A-%27the-power-of-vision%27.

Tanya Jansen, "JFK and the Janitor, the Importance of Understanding the WHY That Is Behind What We Do," *BEQOM*, November 26, 2014, https://www.beqom.com/blog/jfk-and-the-janitor.

Christopher Wren, Lawrence A. Hoffman, and Nancy Wiener, *European Judaism: A Journal for the New Europe*, World Union for Progressive Judaism London Conference (New York: Berghahn Books, 1990).

Tom Junod, "Elon Musk: Triumph of His Will," *Esquire*, November 15, 2012, https://www.esquire.com/news-politics/a16681/elon-musk-interview-1212/.

Casey Crawford, CEO of Movement Mortgage, shared this with me during an in-person interview on February 18, 2018. https://movement.com/.

Roderic Yapp. John Eades, "How Leaders Stack the Deck in Their Favor with Roderic Yapp," *Follow My Lead* podcast, Season 1: Episode 8, July 18, 2016, https://followmylead.libsyn.com/leadership -the-way-its-meant-to-be-with-roderic-yapp.

CHAPTER 7

George Patton. Asad Meah, "35 Inspirational Quotes on Execution," *Awaken the Greatness Within*, https://awakenthegreatnesswithin .com/35-inspirational-quotes-on-execution/.

Bill McDermott, Total Quality Management. Bill McDermott, as told to Drake Baer, "SAP CEO Bill McDermott on the Wisdom of the $99 Suit," *Fast Company*, November 5, 2013, https://www .fastcompany.com/3021059/sap-ceo-bill-mcdermott-on-the -wisdom-of-the-99-suit.

David Schroeder. John Eades, "How to Use Urgency to Thrive as a Leader with David Schroeder," *Follow My Lead* podcast, Season 7: Episode 6, May 2017, https://followmylead.libsyn.com/how-to -thrive-as-a-leader-by-using-urgency-with-david-schroeder.

Dr. Gail Matthews, "Study Shows That Writing Goals Enhances Goal Achievement," Dominican University of California, January 5, 2017, https://www.dominican.edu/dominicannews/study -demonstrates-that-writing-goals-enhances-goal-achievement.

Pareto principle. Vilfredo Pareto, *Cours d'économie politique* (1896), https://en.wikipedia.org/wiki/Pareto_principle.

Mac Lackey. John Eades, "What Moves the Needle with Mac Lackey," *Follow My Lead* podcast, Season 3: Episode 8, 2017, https://followmylead.libsyn.com/what-moves-the-needle-with -mac-lackey.

CHAPTER 8

Dee Ann Turner. John Eades, "It's My Pleasure: Why People and Purpose Matter with Dee Ann Turner," *Follow My Lead* podcast, LearnLoft Season 3: Episode 2, 2017, https://followmylead.libsyn .com/its-my-pleasure-why-people-and-purpose-matter-with-dee -ann-turner

Jimmy Collins., John Eades, "How to Become the Person You Admire with Jimmy Collins," *Follow My Lead* podcast, LearnLoft Season 12: Episode 3, 2017, https://followmylead.libsyn.com/how-to-become-the-person-you-admire-with-jimmy-collins

Amber Selking. John Eades, "Dominate Your Thoughts with Amber Selking," *Follow My Lead* podcast, LearnLoft Season 14: Episode 5, 2018, https://followmylead.libsyn.com/dominate-your-thoughts-with-amber-selking

Eddie Matz, " 'It's Like Group Therapy': How a Rookie Skipper Won Over the Cards' Clubhouse," ESPN, 2018, http://www.espn.com/mlb/story/_/id/24605383/group-therapy-how-rookie-skipper-won-cardinals-clubhouse.

Pat Summitt. "Pat's Definite Dozen," The Pat Summitt Foundation, 1998, http://www.patsummitt.org/our_role/pats_story/pats_definite_dozen.aspx.

CHAPTER 9

King Hammurabi. Evan Andrews, "8 Things You May Not Know About Hammurabi's Code," *History*, December 17, 2013, https://www.history.com/news/8-things-you-may-not-know-about-hammurabis-code.

Mark McGwire. Des Beiler, "Mark McGwire Says He Would Have Hit 70 Home Runs Without PEDs," *Washington Post*, April 9, 2018, https://www.washingtonpost.com/news/early-lead/wp/2018/04/09/mark-mcgwire-says-he-would-have-hit-70-home-runs-without-peds/?noredirect=on&utm_term=.41bc19b81a99.

Magical Feedback research. Daniel Coyle, "The Simple Phrase That Increases Effort 40%," Danielcoyle.com, December 13, 2013, http://danielcoyle.com/2013/12/13/the-simple-phrase-that-increases-effort-40/.

Joe Maddon. Jesse Rogers, "Addison Russell Earns a Bottle of Red from his Manager," ESPN, August 23, 2016, http://www.espn.com/blog/chicago/cubs/post/_/id/40810/addison-russell-earns-a-bottle-of-red-from-his-manager.

Scott Frost. Mitch Sherman, "How Scott Frost Is Transforming Nebraska," ESPN, April 30, 2018, http://www.espn.com/college -football/story/_/id/23339094/how-scott-frost-transforming -nebraska-cornhuskers.

CHAPTER 10

"Brad Stevens" ("Early Life" and "Coaching"), Wikipedia, 2019, https://en.wikipedia.org/wiki/Brad_Stevens.

Brad Stevens, "Two Keys to Leadership," January 9, 2015, https:// www.youtube.com/watch?v=axHQXMtPM7M.

Michael Phelps. "Michael Phelps Biography," Biography.com, last updated 2018, https://www.biography.com/people/michael -phelps-345192.

Alan Stein Jr., "How to Build Winning Habits with Alan Stein Jr.," *Follow My Lead* podcast, LearnLoft Season 9: Episode 7, https:// followmylead.libsyn.com/how-to-build-winning-habits-with -alan-stein-jr

Malcolm Gladwell, *Outliers: The Story of Success* (New York: Little, Brown & Company, 2008).

Anders Ericsson and Robert Pool, *Peak: Secrets from the New Science of Expertise* (New York: Eamon Dolan/Houghton Mifflin Harcourt, 2016).

Whitney Johnson, *Build an A-Team: Play to Their Strengths and Lead Them Up the Learning Curve* (Boston: Harvard Business Review Press, 2018).

F3. "How to Bring Out the Leader Inside of You with F3 Founders Dave Redding and Tim Whitmire," *Follow My Lead* podcast, Season 5: Episode 8, 2018, https://followmylead.libsyn.com/how -to-bring-out-the-leader-inside-of-you-with-f3-founders-dave -redding-and-tim-whitmire.

Matthew Kelly and Patrick Lencioni, *The Dream Manager: Achieve Results Beyond Your Dreams by Helping Your Employees Fulfill Theirs* (New York: Hachette Books, 2007).

Jason Lippert LCI, Dream Achiever Program. Jason Lippert shared this with me during an interview on December 15, 2018.

Lou Holtz, goals. Ryan Connors, "Lou Holtz Goal Setting," Vimeo, 2009, https://vimeo.com/3053900.

David Schwartz, *The Magic of Thinking Big* (Chatsworth, CA: Wilshire Book Co., 1959).

CHAPTER 11

LinkedIn Study. Sarah Lybrand, "Why Recruitment Is the Most Important Business Strategy," May 1, 2018, https://business .linkedin.com/talent-solutions/blog/recruiting-strategy/2018 /what-is-recruitment.

Donald Miller, *Building a StoryBrand: Clarify Your Message So Customers Will Listen* (New York: Thomas Nelson Publishers, 2017).

Albert Mehrabian, *Silent Messages: Implicit Communication of Emotions and Attitude* (New York: Wadsworth Publisher, 1980).

CHAPTER 12

Viktor Frankl, *Man's Search for Meaning* (Beacon Press, 2006).

Urban Meyer, *Above the Line: Lessons in Leadership and Life from a Championship Program* (New York: Penguin Books, 2017).

Marcus Aurelius, *Meditations* (Dover Publications, 1997).

Philip Rivers, "The Latin Phrase That Helped Rivers Begin Again," ESPN, October 14, 2018, http://www.espn.com/videohub/video /clip?id=24979334.

Jay Wright. John Eades, "What the Best Leaders Look for in People with Jay Wright and Jud Linville," *Follow My Lead* podcast, LearnLoft, Season 15: Episode 8, May 2018, https://followmylead .libsyn.com/what-the-best-leaders-look-for-in-people-with-jay -wright-and-jud-linville

Index

refining, 194–195
uncovering, 192–194
Dubey, Abeer, 71–72
Dweck, Carol S., 39

E + R = O (Event + Response =
    Outcome) formula, 219–221
Effort, 60, 222
Eisenhower, Dwight D., xvii, 17,
    50, 123
Elevate leadership style:
  competencies required for, 35–37
  described, 32–33
  team performance associated
    with, 33–35
Elevating others:
  by coaching, 173
  in good leadership, 12, 15–17
  initiative and responsibility for,
    216
  with love and discipline, 22–29
  and PTS Method, 217–218
Elite team culture, 69, 70, 80
Elkind, Peter, 6
E-mail, 59, 159
Emotional (psychological) safety,
    68, 71–72
Emotions:
  decision-making based on,
    203–205
  at Four Stages of Role
    Development, 176–178
Empathy, 36
Empowerment:
  culture of, 65–66
  by frontline managers, 99
  leadership as, 18, 19, 223
Encouragement:
  body language to express, 212
  in coaching, 195–196
  culture of, 65–67, 77
  in Disapproval Dialogues, 157
  of positivity, 78
  in Sustained Excellence stage, 186
Energy:
  as element of culture, 69, 79–82

in elite vs. deficient cultures,
    69, 70
mantras to generate, 79–82
positive, 77, 78
Engagement:
  communication to improve, 211
  and culture, 70
  in meetings, 135–136
Enron Corporation, 6–7
Environment(s):
  collaborative, 72–73
  for disapproval dialogues, 161
  safe, 71–73
  toxic, 7–8, 14–15
Ericsson, Anders, 180–181
Erwin, Mike, 75–76
ESPN, 134
Estill, Jim, 56
Event + Response = Outcome (E +
    R = O) formula, 219–221
Evidence, Direct Dialogue:
  gathering, 150–153
  sharing, 155–156
Exceeding standards:
  in Acts of Accountability model,
    148, 149
  evidence of, 151, 152
  giving praise for, 163–166
Excuses, 159
Expertise, 177, 186

F3 Nation (podcast), 189
F3 (Fitness, Fellowship, and Faith)
    program, 187–190, 196
Failing to meet standards:
  in Acts of Accountability model,
    148, 149
  evidence of, 151, 152
  sharing disapproval over, 154–161
Failure:
  in Building Critical Mass stage,
    183
  in growth mindset, 40
  at leadership, 51, 59–60
  for new managers, xvii
  as part of leadership, 222–223

About the Author

John Eades is an author, podcast host, in-demand speaker, and the CEO of LearnLoft, a leadership development company providing premium content to help elevate the way professionals lead. John and his team at LearnLoft partner with growing companies to power their leadership and culture development initiatives.

Named one of LinkedIn's Top Voices in Management & Leadership, John uses his consistent optimism and research-backed methods to educate and encourage those on their leadership journey. His relentless work ethic and passion for advancing the field of leadership are evident in his writing, videos, and coaching. His blogs, podcasts, and videos have been viewed more than 7 million times and he was awarded a Readership Award by TrainingIndustry.com

John resides in Charlotte, North Carolina, with his wife and two children. He has also achieved success on the golf course—winning the 2019 North Carolina Amateur and the 2017 Carolinas Mid-Amateur.